I0483112

Lean Implementation: Why Lean Fails and How to Prevent Failure

By Ade Asefeso MCIPS MBA

Second Edition

ISBN-13: 978-1499754957

ISBN-10: 1499754957

Publisher: AA Global Sourcing Ltd
Website: http://www.aaglobalsourcing.com

Table of Contents

Disclaimer

This publication is designed to provide competent and reliable information regarding the subject matter covered. However, it is sold with the understanding that the author and publisher are not engaged in rendering professional advice. The authors and publishers specifically disclaim any liability that is incurred from the use or application of contents of this book.

Dedication

To my family and friends who seems to have been sent here to teach me something about who I am supposed to be. They have nurtured me, challenged me, and even opposed me.... But at every juncture has taught me!

This book is dedicated to my lovely boys, Thomas, Michael and Karl. Teaching them to manage their finance will give them the lives they deserve. They have taught me more about life, presence, and energy management than anything I have done in my life.

Part 1: Lean Implementation

Chapter 1: Introduction

So what is "Lean"?

Lean is a series of tools that can be used to improve almost any business process. Those tools are things like 5S, Kaizens, Kan Bans, and Visual Metrics.

Lean is best used to increase capacity. By eliminating wasteful activities, we free up resources that can be used to make more products and services that we can sell. We make more money by selling more stuff. Lean helps us make more stuff with the same people and equipment we already own.

"Lean" is the most widely used buzzword in manufacturing today. (Yeah, this makes me a little unhappy and a little uncomfortable, but I think I can get over it.) Don't let other peoples' misunderstanding of Lean make you think that Lean is not one of the most valuable business concepts you are likely to ever learn.

Henry Ford applied many Lean principles to his assembly line. We have been doing Lean for hundreds of years. But we do have a few twists on these old ideas.

Lean is a philosophy, a set of values, a paradigm, and almost like a religion. Often the benefits of individual Lean activities are very difficult to quantify. Lean works best when it becomes the basis for how you do business. For example: What is the value of your company's business ethics policy? In any one situation, following a code of ethics may hurt your ability to make money. Still, we follow them because they allow us to make the most money in the long run, since no one will routinely deal with an unethical organization. Lean too, pays in the long run, but can actually hurt in the short term.

"Waste": We spend a horrifyingly large amount of time doing wasteful things. Lean helps us to see this waste (which we spent our lifetimes working to hide!), and this lets us get rid of it. Also please notice that "Waste" is in quotations because we have our own, very specific definition of waste which is probably different from your current definition.

"Velocity" and "flow" of materials: We should be able to easily visualize the flow of products and information in our organization. We want this flow to move steadily (and rapidly) through our organization. In a Lean world, we try to reduce the amount of time our materials sit in our factories. We have found that the quicker things move, the easier it is to solve problems and make our processes more efficient. We also crave the ability to immediately see disruptions to this flow, so that we can just as immediately correct those disruptions.

We will never have all the resources we want. Lean helps us free them up from doing non-productive things and lets us redirect them to productive work.

Lean and 6-Sigma go together like peanut butter and jelly. They are very different disciplines, but they dovetail together very well. You will often hear Lean and 6-Sigma described as "Lean Six Sigma" or LSS.

Above all, Lean is simply common sense. Once you have adopted the viewpoint of your customer, all the other Lean concepts are actually pretty simple. If the Lean orthodoxy says you should be doing something one way, but your common sense says you should do it another, follow your common sense. Lean is a tool, and not all tools are usable in all situations. Use your common sense!

Are you looking for a way to increase your profits and create a productive working environment?

Lean manufacturing is one of the best ways to meet customer satisfaction ratings and to strengthen your business as a whole. When you focus on implementing lean manufacturing, you will find ways to reduce wastes and produce higher quality products. This book will offer a simple guide to lean manufacturing so you can get on the fast track to running a successful business.

How does lean manufacturing benefit the customers?

When it comes to proper implementation of lean manufacturing, you are not only thinking about reducing waste for the business, you must also think in terms of your customers. Lean manufacturing provides the customer with a better product for the same or reduced price. The products they are provided are fresh as you no longer keep a large inventory stock on hand. Lean manufacturing involves meeting the demands of the customers and giving them what they want but making sure you are delivering quality to them.

How does lean manufacturing impact the employees?

When you implement lean manufacturing into an organization you are focused on developing stronger relationships with your employees. You are also focused on helping employees to become more productive. Productivity will increase as you work with your employees to clean up their workstations and to fix the defects and loopholes that may occur in your manufacturing processes. Each employee will have a balanced workload so you won't need to worry about employees that seem to have too much work or the employees that seem like they are underutilized. When everyone is able to have a specific workload, their job satisfaction will increase and your company will start to gain higher approval ratings from its employees.

What does lean manufacturing provide to the organization?

Lean manufacturing can improve your production and it will reduce your waste output by 40% or more. The entire program of lean manufacturing is designed to improve the company. Your manufacturing lines will be changed into specific cells so it's easier to identify wastes and problems along the lines of your manufacturing process. Here are a few ways that lean manufacturing will improve your business:

1. **Inventory reduction.** Carrying too much inventory can cause you to tie up your cash reserves and this can cause you to have problems purchasing other equipment and raw goods in the future. Too much inventory also takes up floor space and it can cause your facility to become cluttered, which can lead to workplace accidents.
2. **Overproduction.** This is a big waste to a business as you produce products that won't sell for months or years. The products you produce should only be a few weeks or a few days old when they are sent out to the customers.
3. **Defects.** Lean manufacturing helps to reduce wastes as you will evaluate your machinery and find a way to repair it and to make the overall process run faster. Each cell is in charge of a specific thing so you will be able to dramatically reduce your defect ratio.
4. **Waiting time.** Do you have employees that stand around waiting for a job? What about your machines are they being used the way they should? You need to focus on reducing your waiting time so you aren't wasting money.

These are just a few of the common lean manufacturing principles that you can implement and the results they will bring your company.

Chapter 2: Improve Manufacturing Workflow

If you are a manufacturing business owner it is important to know that the rate that your production process moves along is known as workflow. If the workflow is constantly being interrupted by problems and setbacks then the productivity and the profitability of the entire manufacturing business will be affected. The goal is to have an efficient and smooth workflow.

When your manufacturing workflow is smoother it will also cost your business less, allow you to produce products with higher quality, and in turn make your customers a lot happier. In addition, it has also been shown that when manufacturing businesses have an efficient workflow their employees report higher job satisfaction and morale.

There are many different processes that can help you to improve the workflow within your manufacturing business. However, it is crucial that if you are a manufacturing business owner that you understand that you will need to take the time to learn all you can about each one. You will need to carefully consider which workflow improvement process will work best for your business and the production process that you are currently using.

Manufacturing workflow experts stress that each type of workflow improvement process has both advantages and disadvantages. Here what you need to know to improve manufacturing workflow.

Know that it can be a long, complicated process:

It is important that any manufacturing business owner realize that improving workflow can be a long and complicated process. It most often does not happen overnight. However, the payoff can be so beneficial for your manufacturing business that it is crucial that stick with it. Keep in mind that much of the difficulty results from the fact that there are so many factors to consider in the workflow process. However, if you are careful and concise with your planning you can improve your workflow over time.

Know what workflow improvement process will work for your manufacturing business:

The first step in improving your workflow process is to educate yourself about all of the different workflow processes that are available to use. You must be able to identify if your manufacturing business should use a mass production, series production, or flow production workflow improvement process. Keep in mind that all workflow improvement processes are based on helping you produce more products faster and for a lower cost.

Know that the process will have to applied daily:

It is important to understand that most workflow processes need to be applied everyday. This means that there will always be changes or improvements that you can make to the workflow process. You should also keep in mind that your customer's demands will always be changing which could also necessitate workflow changes and improvements. You should always be considering how your workflow process can be improved in order to bring about a higher degree of customer satisfaction. When you are diligent about making daily workflow improvements you are far more likely to be successful in improving the overall efficiency of the workflow process.

Know that it will have to be constantly monitored:

Manufacturing business owners should keep in mind that this is something that cannot be changed and then left alone. You will need to constantly be looking at the workflow improvements that you have made to determine if they are bringing about an increase in efficiency and productivity. If you fail to do this you will most likely end up having the same workflow problems over and over again. Only by being vigilant about monitoring the workflow process can you be assured that the changes that you have made will bring about improvement and increase the profitability of your manufacturing business.

Chapter 3: Lean Fad

Why is "Lean" still here? Goldratt published "The Goal" in 1984. Womack and Jones published "Lean Thinking" in 1996. Lots of other business fads have come and gone. (Remember "Total Quality Management" or JIT?) Lean by now is the grand old man of business fads. Why is it still here?

Lean is still here because it has been successful, and it has the mixed blessing of being simple enough that most people think they understand it. In fact, almost everybody says they understand Lean. (There probably isn't an engineer in the country who doesn't have "Lean" somewhere on their resume.) It's taught in engineering schools. But unfortunately, this simplicity also means that many people, who think they understand Lean, actually understand "Industrial Engineering". Lean is much, much more than Industrial Engineering, although IE principles are integral to Lean.

What is "Lean Manufacturing" and why should I care?

Lean Manufacturing is a modern approach to manufacturing which attempts to identify and eliminate "waste". Don't let the fancy vocabulary intimidate you. Lean has its origins in ancient Industrial Engineering principles popularized by Henry Ford. In its modern form it was developed by Toyota (think "JIT") and is now used by many manufacturing companies throughout the world (at least, those companies that have a future!). Toyota cleverly called their system "The Toyota Production System" or TPS. Most large manufacturing companies have adopted and adapted TPS, given it some new vocabulary words, and now call it "Lean Manufacturing".

The term "Lean" is very appropriate because Lean Manufacturing focuses on eliminating the "fat" or waste in the manufacturing process. The word "Waste" is defined strictly from the customer's viewpoint as anything that does not add value to the product. In our customer-centric universe, the customer is the sole arbiter of value and non-value; He will only pay for value, and if we offer him non-value, he will take it for free, or go somewhere else.

Exquisitely Simple

The basic ideas in Lean Manufacturing are old, having been well thought out by industrial engineers for almost a century. Don't get hung up trying to follow the orthodoxy; Focus on doing it fast, doing it cheaply, and doing it right the first time. If you apply common sense (which most manufacturing guys have in abundance), you will be doing Lean.

Mundanely Complex

Lean forces you to do your homework. You can't simply tell the people on the floor to go and do something. You have to:
1. Plan how you want him to do it.
2. Understand the flow of materials.

3. Balance the different operations.
4. Write the work instructions.
5. Train him in the process.
6. Continually tell him how he is doing.
7. Satisfy the accountants.

Get your product delivered to the customer when he wants it. If you screw up any of these things, the whole system falls apart. Remember. If it were easy, we did all be doing it already!

Essential for Survival

We British used to have to compete against 63 million fellow British. Like it or not, we are now in a global economy and competing against 6 billion other people. And most of those people are thrilled to work for less than 10% of what we make. Lean is our only hope to beat them!

Chapter 4: Benefits of Using Lean Manufacturing

There are many different benefits for any company that chooses to use lean manufacturing. This manufacturing method has been shown to be one of the most effective ways to reduce waste and improve productivity and profits. Manufacturing business owners find that after they implement lean manufacturing they are spending much less money to produce their products along with producing a higher quality of product. This in turn results in a much higher degree of customer satisfaction. This makes it crucial that every manufacturing business owner understand why they should consider using lean manufacturing. Here are some of the benefits of using lean manufacturing.

Lean manufacturing improves productivity in many different areas of any manufacturing business. These areas include but are not limited to

1. **Human resources:** Human resources is one of the largest costs for any type of business. This is especially true for manufacturing businesses that are highly employee driven. Lean manufacturing helps businesses figure out where their employees will be the most productive. If you have employees who don't know their jobs or simply don't do their jobs well the production process suffers and waste occurs. When lean manufacturing is put into place it can show any problems that are occurring in terms of employees. Then the

manufacturing business owner can determine if employees need to be reassigned to a different jobs, receive additional training, or in some circumstances let go from the manufacturing business.

2. **Production planning:** When manufacturing businesses first implement lean manufacturing this is often the first place that they see major changes. When lean manufacturing is put into place the entire production process becomes more efficient. The production planners will know how much inventory and other supplies that they will need to keep the line moving without risking short outs or spending too much on inventory that is not being used. In addition, problems on the production line will be addressed long before they become large enough to slow down the production process. Orders will be managed in terms of priority and the overall quality of the product(s) that is being produced will go up.

3. **Inventory control:** Many manufacturing business owners overlook the connection between the financial health of their business and their inventory control. The bottom line is that every manufacturing business needs to have exactly the right amount of inventory on hand in order to fill the orders that it has. Lean manufacturing helps to make this happen. When lean manufacturing is used in manufacturing business that means that there is not a large amount of inventory sitting in

the warehouse that is tying up needed cash flow. Lean manufacturing helps manufacturing business owners to keep their inventory at the right amount at all times which improves not only the production process but the financial health of the business, as well.

4. **Time management:** Many manufacturing business owners report that one of the major benefits of using lean manufacturing is the efficient time management that results after the process has begun being used. When lean manufacturing is used it helps to prevent slowdowns on the production line, employees standing around, or gaps in the supply chain that can often happen. Manufacturing business owners realize that their customers value their time as well as their money. Every business owner (regardless of the type of the business), needs to focus on saving their customers time as well as money. When a manufacturing business can meet the needs of their customers on time it means that they will be much happier. This in turn leads to a customer base for the manufacturing business that is full of long term, satisfied customers.

Chapter 5: Why You Need Lean Manufacturing

Waste reduction and the removal of unnecessary process can save companies millions of dollars/pounds a year. Lean manufacturing benefits not only the company but the consumers of the products. The customers get to enjoy increase value to their products while the employees appreciate their jobs due to the incentives and motivational tools used to make the working environment flow better. The purpose of lean manufacturing is to reduce cycle times and get the products to the customers faster than anticipated.

Companies that have small manufacturing defects need to implement lean manufacturing because it will uncover some of these problems and help you come up with solutions for these problems. Anything that doesn't add value to the company, product, or customers will be removed. Using lean manufacturing provides you with a distinct advantage over your competitors since you can product a higher quality product for a lower price.

Lean manufacturing helps to improve the communication process between everyone within the company. When communication breaks down within the company, the manufacturing process will have some hiccups along the way. Lean manufacturing focuses on informing everyone on the supply chain so that they can all come up with the same end result instead of just focusing on one specific task.

The supply chain often has excess waste because people duplicate orders. This leads to waste in time and money for the company not to mention the frustration it causes the employee. The only way to get back on track is to create a smooth work-flow, which requires proper communication with the supply chain. The supply chain is in charge of several things that impact your bottom line including:
1. Transportation
2. Machine set-up
3. Inventory
4. Quality consistency and inspection
5. Material handling

Lean manufacturing not only helps to improve the different process it also finds ways to make use of wasted space. If you have small spaces that are not being used, you can do small things to make use of it. Perhaps moving some equipment around or moving parts to this area will improve the flow of production. Lean manufacturing also helps to improve delivery time, defects, handling of materials, and storage requirements. Since products are made to order, it makes it easier for companies to use their employees and equipment effectively. You no longer will leave machines on when they are not being used and you won't pay your employees to sit around and watch television or read magazines while they wait until the inventory is sold before the start producing products.

Companies that implement lean manufacturing produce higher-quality products for lower prices. This allows them to market their products faster and control their marketing and advertising costs. Proper control over your cash flow will help you with company expansion and development.

Implementing lean manufacturing helps to get rid of most of the manufacturing challenges your company may be experiencing. If you have watched the process and you can't find the inefficiencies, lean manufacturing will help you identify them. You can then develop a method to solve the problem and prevent them from occurring in the future.

Lean manufacturing helps to smooth out business processes between all departments. Here are some other ways lean manufacturing will improve your company:
1. Reduced cycle times.
2. Improved customer satisfaction.
3. Reduced administrative costs.
4. Waste reduction.
5. Generating profits by removing unnecessary processes.
6. Better control over the day-to-day operations of the company.
7. Reduces competition from other companies.
8. Promotes friendly office practices.

Lean manufacturing is a process and it takes time to completely master it.

Chapter 6: Using Kaizen Methodology to Reduce Waste

Manufacturing organizations deal with waste on a daily basis. Waste could include idle time of equipment, idle time of employees, and some of the more common thought of actual wasted product, defects, recalls, shipment issues, so on and so forth. Studies show that Manufacturing companies waste over 70% of their resources, while those who implement Lean Manufacturing cut that percentage in half.

Kaizen methodology deals with change. It is a philosophy of continuous change for improvement. Kaizen requires a set standard for high quality, companywide involvement from all employees, effort from all employees top to bottom, a willingness to change and do things differently, and most importantly communication.

Involving all employees to help better their work environment improves morale and gives each employee a personal stake in the company. Set up a method to acquire suggestions and ideas, analyze, and then implement.

Standardize your processes. Set up guidelines that must be followed. Get feedback on how these standardized processes are working and analyze them. Don't limit yourself to one method of operation. You may find that there may be a better process. If you find a better way, change the standard.

Come up with a concise housekeeping policy. Sort your product in the most effective manner. Being organized reduces time and effort in finding material. Ensure that all areas are cleaned and swept continuously. Maintaining a clean area is not only more efficient, it is safer.

In order for Kaizen to work properly, you must implement the 3 following principles:
1. First, you must consider the process and the results. The process and results will surface the actions needed to achieve the correct results.
2. Second, you must have a systematic thinking of the entire process instead of just the immediate problems. This is simply to avoid creating or missing problems in other parts of the process.
3. Third, you need to approach kaizen with a non-judgmental, non-blaming, and learning method. This allows for the re-examination of assumptions that were part of the current process.

Kaizen can be implemented on an individual level or it can be used within large and small groups. Kaizen works by making changes and monitoring the results and then making necessary adjustments. Obviously, the Toyota Production System is known for using kaizen. Within Toyota, all personnel are expected to stop moving production lines if there is any slight notification of abnormalities. The employee is then expected to suggest an improvement to resolve the abnormality (this initiates kaizen).

Once kaizen is implemented, it is up to management to improve and maintain it. Maintenance is about maintaining the current managerial, technological, and operating standards. Improvement focuses on improving the current standards. With kaizen thinking, the maintenance function will establish a set of rules, policies, directives, and standard operating procedures.

From here, management must make everyone work at following the standard operating procedures. Typically this assignment is given to human resources to develop a letter that will site discipline for failure to adhere to the standard operating procedures. As far as improvement goes, management will always go towards revising the current standards and establishing better ones. Kaizen uses small improvements over a specific period of time and result in coordinated continuous efforts by every employee at the company.

In western culture, Kaizen is often referred to as "continuous process improvement". Instead of taking a stern approach against defects, continuous process improvement focuses on inspiring employees to work harder and work together to achieve the same end result. Employees must have a change of attitude and learn new ways to perform their job duties. Proper implementation of kaizen will reduce wastes and improve your company's production performance.

34

Chapter 7: Kaizen Blitz

So you want to start getting the benefits of Lean now. One of the best ways to quickly begin the transition to Lean is to run a series of Kaizen Blitzes.

The word "Kaizen" is from the Japanese words "kai" (change) and "zen" (to a goal). "Blitz" of course, is from the German for "lightning". A Kaizen Blitz is a rapid change for the better.

Here is how they are typically done

A cross-functional team is assembled, consisting of people working in the area to be improved, and at least one person not working in the area. The team also consists of a variety of professional skills, such as operator, manager, mechanic, engineer, and accountant.

The leadership of the team consists of:
1. A Team Leader who keeps the whole group focused.
2. An assistant Team Leader who is a future Team Leader in training.
3. An Instructor (often the Team Leader).

The team is excused from their normal duties for the duration of the blitz, which is usually 3 to 5 days. It is very important that the team members concentrate on the blitz, and not their usual jobs. Sometimes, the blitz is scheduled so that the team members have a few hours before or after the blitz each day to handle the normal emergencies. However, while the blitz is underway, the team needs to ignore their normal jobs and focus exclusively on the blitz.

The team receives formal instruction in Lean Manufacturing principles and the methodology of the Blitz on the first day. The Lean principles' training always emphasizes the specific skills needed to execute the blitz. For example, if this is a 5S Blitz, then specific information about 5S is presented during the training session.

The team formally determines the goals of the Blitz. Often the goals are decided by the Blitz Leader and simply presented to the team for acknowledgement.

The team spends time formally evaluating the current situation. This means they perform a survey of the cell as it is today, giving a numerical score if possible. This evaluation will be duplicated at the end of the Blitz to determine how effective the Blitz was.

After the evaluation is complete, the team meets to plan the improvements they wish to make. They may split into sub-groups to attack specific areas or perform specific tasks.

The team then spends several days actually making the improvements. To keep their focus, means are typically brought in so the team can spend most of its time working the Blitz.

At the end of the Blitz period, the team conducts another formal evaluation and then compares the beginning and ending conditions.

Most Blitz teams will have a few uncompleted tasks left over. These tasks are added to a "newspaper" of work to be done over the next few weeks.

Finally, the team creates a presentation of their results and presents it to the plant's managers. This gives the managers an opportunity to show their support for the efforts of the team, and to publicly praise the results.

Types of Blitzes

A Kaizen Blitz process can be used to make almost any type of rapid improvement. However, they usually fall under one of the following types:
1. 5S implementation
2. TPM implementation
3. Kan Ban or Pull System implementation
4. Value Stream Map creation or revision
5. Setup Time Reduction
6. Quality Problem resolution
7. Process Variation reduction

Why Blitzes Fail

The Kaizen Blitz process is not perfect, and does not work every time. When it fails, it usually does so for one of the following reasons:
1. Lack of true support or commitment from the participants or management.

2. Scope too large to be completed in 3 - 5 days.
3. Lack of follow-up on newspaper items.
4. The wrong team members (i.e.: The team members are not people who are close to the problem)

Kaizen 10 Commandments

1. Solve the problem once. Find the root cause and correct it, not the symptom.
2. Don't think of reasons why it won't work. Figure out ways to make it work.
3. Don't blame anyone for the current situation; improve it!
4. Don't wait for perfection. A small improvement done now is worth more than a big improvement done later.
5. Don't take anybody's word. See it with your own eyes. Get the facts.
6. Don't spend a lot of money. Most good improvements are very low cost.
7. Wisdom arises from difficulty; consider difficulty a challenge to overcome.
8. Ask "why?" at least 5 times.
9. The wisdom of the entire team is more valuable than the knowledge of any one person.
10. You can always make improvements every time you try.

Chapter 8: Kaizen Event Structure

Having selected the problem and chartered the team the Kaizen Event is typically conducted over a five-day period as outlined below:

Day 1: Plan

1. Training on Lean principles, concepts, techniques, and tools pertinent to the problem to be resolved.
2. Observation of the current condition to collect and validate the data underlying the problem.
3. Witness the issues contributing to the problem directly.

Day 2: Plan - Do

1. Start to implement counter measures that address the root-cause of the problems found.

Day 3: Plan - Do - Check

1. Validate the counter measures.
2. Implement new counter measure if the initial ones are not effective.
3. Continue to experiment until a validated solution is identified.

Day 4: Plan -Do - Check - Act

1. Establish "Standard Work" for all validated solutions.

Day 5: Share and Celebrate

1. Present output to the management, customer and suppliers.
2. Identify cross-deployment opportunities.
3. Recognise the contribution of the team by respecting their achievements.

It is our experience that the above approach has delivered improvements to key metrics ranging from 30-60%. This is often achieved at the same time as developing the capability to apply Lean Tools that can be re-used again and again to other metrics across the value stream.

Chapter 9: Overall Equipment Effectiveness

Overall Equipment Effectiveness (OEE) is a "best practices" way to monitor and improve the efficiency of a Manufacturing processes (i.e. machines, manufacturing cells, assembly lines). It can also be used to discover and resolve bottlenecks or aid an organization in inexpensively tapping into an area that has excess capacity.

Once planned shutdown time (e.g. planned breaks, maintenance etc) has been subtracted from plant operating time (the time the facility is open and available for equipment operation) one arrives at planned production time. Any losses in planned production time can then be categorized into 3 elements. These are as follows:

1. Availability (Downtime)

Availability losses include any downtime losses which include any event that stops planned production. Examples of availability losses include equipment failure, material shortages and changeover times. Result is calculated as the ratio of Operating time to Planned Production time.

2. Performance (Speed loss)

Performance losses take into account losses associated when the equipment/department operates at lower than optimal speed when running. Examples include machine wear, substandard materials, misfeeds and operator efficiency.

Result is calculated as the ratio of Net Operating time (Operating time minus downtime) to Operating time.

3. Quality (Quality loss)

Quality losses address reject or poor quality work which will need subsequent processing or rework to correct.

Result is calculated as the ratio of Full Productive time (Net Operating time minus Speed Loss) and Net Operating time.

The OEE index is calculated as the product of the above three, i.e. OEE index = % Availability x %Performance x %Quality.

It is very important to recognize that improving OEE is not the only objective. Take a look at the following data for two production shifts.

OEE Factor	Shift 1	Shift 2
Availability	90.0%	95.0%
Performance	95.0%	95.0%
Quality	99.5%	96.0%
OEE	85.1%	86.6%

Superficially, it may appear that the second shift is performing better than the first, since its OEE is higher. Very few companies, however, would want to trade a 5.0% increase in Availability for a 3.5% decline in Quality!

The beauty of OEE is not that it gives you one magic number; it's that it gives you three numbers, which are all useful individually as your situation changes from day to day. And it helps you visualize performance in simple terms; a very practical simplification.

Example OEE Calculation

The table below contains hypothetical shift data, to be used for a complete OEE calculation, starting with the calculation of the OEE Factors of Availability, Performance, and Quality. Note that the same units of measurement (in this case minutes and pieces) are consistently used throughout the calculations.

Item	Data
Shift Length	8 hours = 480 min.
Short Breaks	2 @ 15 min. = 30 min.
Meal Break	1 @ 30 min. = 30 min.
Down Time	47 minutes
Ideal Run Rate	60 pieces per minute
Total Pieces	19,271 pieces
Reject Pieces	423 pieces

Planned Production Time   =   Shift   Length   -
Breaks
            = 480 - 60
            = 420 minutes

Operating Time   = Planned Production Time -
Down Time
            = 420 - 47
            = 373 minutes

Good Pieces   = Total Pieces - Reject Pieces
            = 19,271 - 423
            = 18,848 pieces

Availability   =   Operating   Time   /   Planned
Production Time
            = 373 minutes / 420 minutes
            = 0.8881 or 88.81%

Performance   =   (Total   Pieces/Operating   Time)
/Ideal Run Rate
            =(19,271pieces/373minutes)/60pieces
per minute
            = 0.8611 or 86.11%

Quality   = Good Pieces / Total Pieces
            = 18,848 / 19,271 pieces
            = 0.9780 or 97.80%

OEE   = Availability x Performance x Quality
            = 0.8881 x 0.8611 x 0.9780
            = 0.7479 or 74.79%

In terms of outcome, and OEE index of 100% represents perfection.

The OEE index is frequently used as a key metric in TPM (Total Productive Maintenance) and Lean Manufacturing programs. It is simple to implement and very practical. While it is easily calculated, it is a very powerful metric for comparative purposes and is also very useful for monitoring improvements in a continuous improvement programme.

Chapter 10: Value Stream Mapping

One of the tools used in Six Sigma is called value stream mapping. Value stream mapping allows you to see where your company is at now and where your company is headed. This allows you to plan for large customer demands and to prepare for times when customer demand is minimal. Value stream mapping is easy to implement and it provides companies with a great view of their manufacturing processes.

From the outside view, value stream mapping is extremely complicated. The map actually shows a connection from each individual component in the process along with their relationships to one another. The map will help you look over every process and look for some of the hidden wastes that exist.

Since most people are visual learners, value stream mapping provides them with a visual way to view productivity and performance. The map allows everyone at the company to see the same thing and correspond with one another.

Another benefit of value stream mapping is that it also allows you to map the existing processes to gain a view of how things are currently working. You can immediately see things that can be changed to quickly improve the company. Since you have instant results, you can discuss some changes that will impact your company into the distant future or just small departments within the company. The changes will go into effect immediately so the value stream map will reveal the results within a few days.

It is difficult to make predictions for the future and map them, which is why many companies only use value stream mapping for their present state. Comparing current results to future predictions often leads to disconnection between departments. This is due to the fact that some departments rely heavily on others and if they disagree with their predictions, it will cause problems for their department.

Every employee will have a unique role in value stream mapping and proper implementation of Six Sigma. Since the goal of the process is to reduce inefficiencies and improve performance, it is important for every employee to take steps toward improving their work performance. Quite often it boils down to the way they think about their job and the way they carry out certain job duties. If you find that they mundanely walk through their job duties, they are producing waste somewhere. The goal of Six Sigma is to help get them motivated and involved in the process. Employees must have a voice in mapping the future of the company.

Proper implementation of Six Sigma will improve employee morale and increase your sales. Companies that use value stream mapping are able to view some of the common lean manufacturing programs the company has tried and if they have been helpful. You can then compare them to some of the tools used in conjunction with Six Sigma to see the results.

Chapter 11: Hidden Waste

Manufacturing is a complex business that can produce a number of different wastes. Waste is considering anything that does not add value to the finished product. The basis of efficient manufacturing is finding the waste that is occurring in the manufacturing setting and dealing with it. While some waste is fairly obvious there are other types of waste that can seem more hidden. Savvy manufacturing business owners will do all they can to seek out these wastes and eliminate them from the production process. When these wastes have been eliminated the manufacturing company will be able to produce a higher quality of product for a lower cost. This in turn will make their customers happier and more satisfied which will increase productivity.

Here is what you need to know about manufacturing wastes you may not be aware of:

Making too much

If you are overproducing your product then you are creating waste. If can't generate enough sales for what you are making then you are simply making too much and wasting your resources. You want to do everything you can to avoid having inventory sitting in your warehouse or on your shelves.

Taking too long

If you find that you have employees standing around or processes that are delaying production then you have waste. Keep in mind that you are paying those employees even if they are doing nothing! This makes it crucial that you understand that if you have to spend any time waiting for anything then you are wasting time which is the same as wasting money.

Shipping it wrong

Transportation can be a huge cost for many manufacturing businesses. This is true whether you are talking about in-house shipping or delivering to your customers. If you are spending too much on any kind of shipping or the shipping that you are doing is causing delays then you have waste. Manufacturing business owners will need to take very close look at how everything is moved within and outside of their business.

Working too hard

When your employees are working to hard this means they are over processing. If your employees must spend an inordinate amount of time producing a particular product this is waste as well. Your production line should be efficient enough that there is no one single product that takes more time and effort than something else.

Having too much

This type of waste refers to inventory control. You want to make sure that your cash flow is not tied up in your inventory. If you have too much inventory you are simply wasting money on inventory that is just sitting. Manufacturing business owners need to focus on maintaining enough inventory to avoid line stoppage while not having inventory that is just sitting.

Moving too much

If you have too many processes on your production line or overly complicated processes this is waste and must be corrected. You want to make sure that your production process is as streamlined as possible. This can be done by carefully studying the production line and making sure that no one has to do more than necessary to produce a particular product.

Producing faulty products

Defective products can be a huge waste for any manufacturing business. It is crucial to make sure that you have implemented the processes necessary to reduce the amount of defective products that your business makes. When you have a large amount of defective products it takes up valuable resources dealing with them and everything should be done to avoid this. In addition, you need to make sure that your employees are trained well enough that this kind of waste can be reduced.

Chapter 12: 7 Deadly Wastes

Fundamentally, Lean Manufacturing defines a toolbox of tools to use that can help to eliminate "waste". This waste is generally fit into 7 (+1) categories. These are:

Defects

The normal type of waste we've known all along. We call it scrap. Our existing factory procedures and systems are well equipped to identify, track, and correct this type of waste.

Overproduction

If you make it faster or sooner than the customer wants it, you've wasted your resources. Ideally, we make things at the exact rate that the customer wants them (his "takt" time). Any overproduction is waste. For old-time production guys, this can be a very difficult concept to accept.

Waiting

The most obvious form of waste (and therefore, my favourite), waiting is anathema to almost everyone on the shop floor. This is the best form of waste to have, precisely because it is so visible, and visible waste is the easiest to eliminate.

Inventory

The form of waste that the accountants love; (Or at least they used to love it before they became enamoured of "Working Capital".) They call it an asset, but we know it really is a liability. It cost money to make, hasn't generated a dime for us yet (we haven't sold it yet), and has a nasty habit of being damaged or becoming obsolete. Old timers love it because it may have saved their butts once, but the problems it causes far outweigh the rare benefits it occasionally provides.

Processing

This refers to the extra stuff we do to the product that the customer doesn't want or care about. Examples include: 1) Inspection, 2) Rework, 3) Sorting, etc etc.

Conveyance

This is a fancy word for "picking' it up and moving' it". The most obvious form is the forklift that carries things around the factory. It may be hard to believe, but the customer doesn't care how many times you picked it up and moved it; he is only interested in the product being where he wants it at the end.

Motion

This refers to unneeded motions of people and products, and includes the classic "mechanic walking to get a tool for a setup". Good 5S can help eliminate this form of waste.

Unused Talent

The 8th of the 7 Deadly Wastes; "From the neck down is minimum wage." You've hired their bodies; don't forget their minds!

A truly Lean enterprise scrounges for every resource it can find, and uses it all aggressively. Even the dumbest guy on the shop floor is an expert at something. Make him an ally, and get him to implement his own good ideas!

Chapter 13: How to Get Ready for 5S Implementation

When you are working on creating a solid manufacturing plant, there are many different things that you need to consider. You need to be able to consider looking into the issues that are related to your organization from product defects to employee morale issues. These issues need to be easy to identify so that you can select a program that will work effectively at reducing issues to waste and other concerns. The 5S method is one of the most popular because of how easy it is to implement but also due to how it has a positive impact on the company.

Proper implementation of the 5S method will come down to having a raise in employee morale along with an increase in overall productivity and customer satisfaction levels. When you are dealing with any type of implementation of a new product you need to be able to look at some important characteristics like how management approaches the program. Management needs to be able to deal with the program in teaching your employees about what to do with the program and they need to see that management is behind the program. Management needs to be able to support the program for it to work.

The 5S method is something that you need to be educated about. It is a good idea to consider attending training seminars and other things as this can help you to learn about different implementation methods and will also give you assistance in how to pitch it to your company. When you approach the program in the right way, people are not as resistant to it.

The biggest thing to remember when you are dealing with 5S is being able to handle the problems that are related to your employee's personalities and resistance to the program. Employees always have resistance to change. They have a hard time being able to understand it and how it works and they want to be able to know that it can work but they need to see that it can work in the right way where it's not going to have a big impact on their job. Explain to them how the program is going to work and how it can save the company money, which will end up coming back to the employees in their pay cheques.

A great way to help your employees to be able to understand the program is by having it implemented through teams. Teamwork is a great way to help you understand how everyone can work together to make the program successful. What can employees do that can contribute? Give them a chance to come up with their own ideas and other things as this will be able to make it much easier on them to focus on creating an effective program.

For the 5S method to work, everyone needs to be able to pull their own weight. You all need to be able to sustain the parts that you are responsible for and to have everyone on the team be in charge of certain workstations and other things. Hold meetings so you can have everyone in charge of different areas of the 5S program. When you have the program implemented in the proper way and you have it focused on continual improvements it will start to show progress. Patience is the key to being successful with 5S as you need to focus on giving the program time to work. It is not something that will happen overnight, it will take time and substantial effort on your part to work as everyone at the company needs to stay focused on the program and making it a success.

Chapter 14: Why 5S Method Tops the Class

There are a number of different ways in which you can focus on improving the various manufacturing processes within your organizations. Lean manufacturing is one of the best ways to improve your manufacturing processes using different approaches like the 5S methodology. The 5S method is one of the most popular as you can create it and mould it into several different ways to make it work correctly for whatever type of business you have.

The 5S method comes from the following:
1. Sort
2. Set In Place
3. Shine
4. Standardize
5. Sustain

This system is popular mostly because it will help to organize a business. This will make it easier on everyone to have a role in it and this creates a cleaner, more productive working environment. Some companies will employ all of the 5S method at one time while others will take time to start small and just do one step at a time. Since the entire system is all combined, it is pretty easy to get it done all at once.

Since the S method is so easy to implement, it makes it one of the best methods to start with if you would like to eliminate waste and to improve your overall manufacturing process. Here are the steps to follow when you are implementing the 5S method.

Sort

This is the first step which is where you will basically organize the company. You will go through all of the different areas and start getting rid of all the unnecessary items that are simply taking up too much room on your shop floor or even on your desks. Unnecessary items will cause clutter and it makes it very difficult for you to be productive as too many things are slowing you down. In the sort phase you will tag all of the items and move them to another area where you can look over them and decide if you would like to eliminate them or just keep them in a storage box.

Set in Place

How many items are not organized? Do you have boards where tools should be held and they are missing? The Set in Place phase will be able to help you maximize the efficiency of your company as you have all the materials in place and they are easy to find. Shadow boards are the most common method that are used in this phase.

Shine

This phase is where you will end up cleaning your entire company. You need to do a deep cleaning where you have all the machines cleaned up and ready for use. With the shine phase you need to work on quality and efficiency so that it will not allow your machinery to deteriorate over time.

Standardize

This is the phase where you create a process that will standardize the entire company. It can be hard to do as everyone needs to get on board with the system but it can be done with the right type of leaders and the implementation phase. Never forget this phase because it is the vital phase. Some companies are great with the first 3 phases but they do not take the time to do the last 2 phases, which are necessary in order to have long-term improvements.

Sustain

This is your final phase where you will spend time maintaining everything that you have learned. You must take time to keep the company lean and to ensure the new process is carried out correctly. There are a lot of people that get lazy on this phase and do not do it. If you don't sustain, all the hard work you went through was all for not.

Chapter 15: Using 5S Method

Reducing waste and improving manufacturing processes is at the top of the list for many companies that are trying to save money. Most people will use Six Sigma or TQM to improve the way their business currently runs. One of the most effective tools of a process improvement strategy is the 5 "S" method.

The 5 "S" method is used with lean manufacturing to teach employees how to organize their workstations. Proper implantation of the 5 "S" method will improve efficiency, product quality, and it helps to improve safety. The 5 "S" method is broken down as follows:

Sort (Seiri)

This is the first S. It focuses on eliminating unnecessary items from the workplace. This is when you sort through all the tools and materials in the work environment and eliminate the unused ones. You will keep only used tools. Quite often this process is known as red tagging.

A red tag is placed on all the items that are not needed to complete your job. If you do not discard the items, you will move them to a holding area. The reason for this is to evaluate the red tag items for future use. Some used items are moved to a warehousing facility while other items may be discarded. Sorting eliminates broken tools, obsolete materials, and raw scrap materials. This allows you to free up valuable space.

Set In Order (Seiton)

This the second S. Set in order focuses on effective storage methods and efficiency. Set in order is often called straighten because it is the process of arranging tools and equipment after a manner that promotes effective work flow. There are a few questions you need to ask yourself when you are implementing set in order:

1. What tools do I need in order to effectively do my job?

2. Where should the tools I need be kept?

3. How many of these tools do I need in order to do my job?

Some strategies for set in order include outlining work areas and locations, painting floors, modular shelving and cabinets, and shadow boards. Think about how having a designated "cleaning closet" will save you time when you are looking for a broom or a mop. By having a designated area for everything, you will eliminate wasted time by your employees as they search for items.

Shine (Seiso)

After you have followed set in order and sort, the next s is shine or sweeping. The clutter and junk should be eliminated by this point and the next process is to thoroughly clean the work environment. The workplace needs to be kept clean and neat in order to be efficient. Daily follow-up cleaning will be necessary in order to maintain the improvement levels you have set in place. Daily cleaning will be a part of the work required, not just an occasional activity when the work environment is too messy. Your workers should take pride in a clean and clutter-free work environment.

The shine or sweeping step will create ownership to your employees for their area and the equipment they use. The shine phase will also unveil underlying problems such as leaks, broken equipment, fatigue, contamination, vibration, and misalignment. Obviously if these small problems go unnoticed, it could lead to larger problems such as equipment failure and loss of production. In the end, it will affect your bottom line.

Standardize (Seiketsu)

This means that everyone must know their role. The fourth s concentrates on making employees practice the best standardized rules for their area. The employees can be involved in the development of these standardized rules because they are valuable for the information they deal with on a day to day basis. In the end, everyone should know exactly what their job responsibilities are and they should know exactly how to perform them.

Sustain (Shitsuke)

This refers to maintaining and reviewing standards. This is the most difficult s to implement and achieve.

Implementing change is hard for many individuals to accept. More often than not, change will occur for a small time period and people will revert back to their old ways, where they feel comfortable. Once you have established the first four s's, they are the new way of operating. You must put steps in place to avoid a gradual decline of the new rules to adjust back to the old way of operating. If an issue does arise, such as a suggested improvement or a new way of operating, then a review of the first four s's is appropriate.

Just remember that you need to define the new operating system and set standards so that the workplace stays organized and avoids reverting to old behaviours.

Chapter 16: Where to Begin Lean Journey

As many organizations attempt to become "World Class Manufacturing" operations, where to begin their lean journey is the first question facing management. The answer for many is a 5S program. The 5s's are: sort, set in order, shine, standardize, and sustain. Depending on a company's situation, 5S can be implemented in different ways. However, many companies have found success using the following 8 steps:

1. Organize the program committee.

2. Develop a plan for each S.

3. Publicly announce the start of the program.

4. Provide training and education to employees.

5. Select a day in which everybody cleans up his/her own working area.

6. Select a day in which everybody organizes his/her own working area.

7. Evaluate the results of 5S.

8. Perform Self-Examination and Take Corrective Actions.

5S, like all other quality and prevention initiatives, requires commitment from top management and participation by everyone in the organization. Requiring plans tailored to each facility, a 5S program cannot be implemented using a "one-size-fits-all" approach. 5S is best implemented very gradually over a period of time. Because implementing five S can be such an overwhelming task, some companies decide to institute it department-by-department.

The most common mistake companies make when implementing 5S is the failure to train adequately at the outset. Upper management and other members of the steering group must have a working knowledge of 5S. This starts with a thorough review of the 5S program, implementation methods, team concepts, and the role of management. Practical exercises, or a real world pilot project, should follow. Since most steering group members work in the office, they should also apply 5S to their own office or work area. This activity will not only provide a practical understanding of 5S and the kinds of issues that will need to be addressed throughout the implementation, but it also communicates the commitment of upper management to a company-wide 5S implementation. At this point, management should endorse the formal Five S plan and set dates for implementation.

The implementation team, typically consisting of supervisors and team leaders, is the next group to be trained. Requiring the same training as upper management plus training in team leadership, they should receive practical training through the implementation of pilot projects. A good approach is to carry out one pilot program under the leadership of the 5S advisor (a consultant or internal resource fully experienced in all aspects of 5S) and then to carry out a second one on their own. A program committee that includes the plant manager and some of the area workers should coordinate the preliminary work. Once the preliminary work is completed, plans describing implementation of the Five S campaign should be prepared and released. When the results are satisfactory, the program can then be launched company wide.

The goal and process of the first "S" is organization. The sort process distinguishes needed items from unneeded items and removes the latter. This process forces people to remove all items not currently needed for work, whether they are in the factory or in the office. It is initially the most difficult for people who are afraid to let go of parts, machines, and data "just in case" they may be needed in the future. However, "red-tagging" items allow workers to set aside and evaluate items and information in terms of their usefulness and frequency of use.

The items and information are returned, stored elsewhere, sold, given away, or thrown away. Red tagging is best done in one target area at a time and within one or two days. When red tagging is completed, problems and annoyances in the workflow are reduced, communication between workers is improved, product quality is increased, and productivity is enhanced.

"Set in order" organizes a work area for the maximum possible efficiency. Organization and orderliness work best when they are implemented together. "Set in order" means arranging needed items so that they are easy to use and labelling them so that anyone can find them and put them away. The key word in this definition is "anyone." Labelling is mostly for other people who need what is in the area, when the area "owner" is away. The benefit is economy of time and motion. When orderliness is implemented, there is no wasted human energy or excess inventory.

"Shine" - as the word implies - means to thoroughly clean everything in the work area. Planning a cleanliness campaign is a five-step process including:
1. Cleanliness targets.
2. Assignments.
3. Methods.
4. Tools.
5. Follow-up inspections.

The goal is threefold:
1. To turn the workplace into a clean, bright place where people enjoy working.
2. To review the first two Ss.
3. To find the source of dirt or litter and eliminate it.

The definition of cleanliness is "keeping everything swept and clean." "Shine" should become so deeply ingrained as a daily work habit that tools are also kept in top condition and are ready for use at any time.

Once the first three "S's" are in place, "standardize" details a plan to maintain the continual improvement activities. The plan should include the creation of procedures and simple daily checklists that are to be visibly posted in each work area; the checklist should serve as a visual to ensure that the daily 5S requirements are being met. Standardized cleanup integrates sort, set in order, and shine into a unified whole.

The last "S," sustain, requires discipline. Without discipline, it is impossible to maintain consistent standards of quality, safety, clean production, and process operation. The more closely workers are able to follow manufacturing standards, procedures, and rules, the less likelihood there is of errors, defects, waste, and accidents. However, trying to impose discipline in an authoritarian manner will not get far in most firms today. Rather, people should be motivated to want to follow the rules because the workplace rules are actually a set of shared values.

Shared values are achieved by coaching and team participation, not by orders and penalties. Implementation of 5S provides coaching by getting the workers to do the simple things right. "Buying in" to these basic values is the essential starting point to developing a "World Class" organization. Empowering shop floor workers to take control of their daily activities and their work environment is the unifying principle of 5S. By taking an active role in designing and maintaining their workplace, workers take more pride in their work, leading to greater satisfaction and higher productivity.

Many believe that 5S is a must have tool. For any of the tools in the toolkit for becoming lean, quick changeover, total productive maintenance, mistake proofing, and so on. 5S significantly helps in both the implementation and sustaining of improvements. The Gold Standard for 5S is that anyone should be able to find anything in their own workplace in less than 30 seconds, and anywhere else in the workplace in less than 5 minutes without talking to anyone, opening a book, or turning on a computer. 5S is the foundation for successful lean implementation. 5S is the tool to begin, support, and sustain the lean journey.

Chapter 17: Power of the 5S

5S is the single most critical component of Lean Manufacturing. If you do nothing else for Lean, do 5S. All the lean disciplines flow from 5S, and without a solid 5S foundation, all the lean activities you implement will slowly wither away.

5S refers to 5 Japanese words that begin with the "S" sound. The English equivalents are "Sort", "Set in order", "Shine", "Standardize", and "Sustain".

5S always starts with cleaning up and painting lines on the floor, and many people therefore think that 5S is "cleaning up", but it is much more. The most important part of 5S is the "Standardization" that allows for all future improvements.

Why 5S?

Have you ever been looking for a spare part to a machine that just went down, and you know that you have it, but you can't find it?

We want a well 5S'd operation for many reasons. The most important reason is that it helps us be more efficient and reduces the total waste. Imagine that you are trying to find the alien hiding in your kid's closet, but you can't because he is got too many stuffed toys. The same thing happens when you are looking for that important spare part that will get your important machine back to work. 5S saves us money.

The S's

Sort Through and Sort Out

The first step to 5S is to get rid of things that should not be present in the work area. If you are keeping things around because you think they may someday be useful, think again. In a well 5S'd world, only those items which are used on a regular basis should be nearby. Things which are used less often should be stored far away, while things that are used frequently should be very close. For example, the screw driver you use every 5 minutes should be stored on a hook on your belt, while the special calibration fixture which you use once a year should be labelled and stored in a distant warehouse.

Rule of Thumb

If you haven't used it for 30 days and you don't know when you will use it again... Remove it!

But wait! What if you find out next week you needed the thing you just threw away? This is going to happen. You will do a major 5S, and throw away a ton of old stuff, and then someone (usually the boss) will irately demand to know why you threw away the item he is signing a purchase requisition for. The short answer is that it is worth it to buy back the 5% of what you threw away to clear out the 95% you don't need. Also, we use a "Red Tag" system to give everybody a chance to see and claim what we feel we don't need.

Don't let the packrats rule! "When in doubt, throw it out!"

An example of why 5S is so powerful.

I do not know where all of the pictures in this book were taken. (I received them from a trainer several years ago.) This is an excellent example of the power of 5S.

1st S - Sort

BEFORE   AFTER

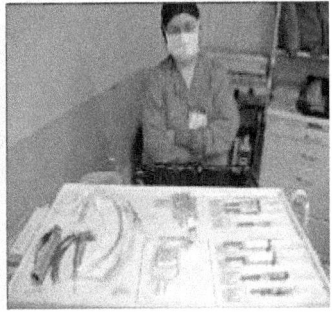

"A Place for everything, and everything in its place."

Once you've gotten rid of stuff you don't need, you need to put the stuff you want where you want it. Don't get hung up finding the "perfect" place; the most important thing is to pick a specific place and then use it. (You will almost certainly will find a new, better place sometime in the future.) As you select places for items in the workplace, keep in mind the rules about frequently used items being close, and infrequently used items being far away.

2nd S - Set In Order

This step is important because it eliminates the various types of waste that were previously identified, and prevents or reduces the types of errors previously identified. When you apply this step you create a place for everything and put everything in the correct place. Another way to think about this is you are creating Standardization. A consistent way to work.

Visual Controls are created in this step to assist with standardization. A visual control is any communication device used to inform anyone at a glance how work is and should be done. It can communicate many types of information such as where things belong, how many of those things are needed at that location, what the standard operating procedure is for restocking, and other types of information that it useful in the workflow.

How to Set In Order

Set in order by finding the best location for the items, supplies and equipment that you have determined that you need in the workplace. Think through the flow of work to help to determine the best location.

1. Locate items in terms of their frequency of use so store the ones used the most near the place where they are used.
2. Store items together if they are used together.
3. Store them in the sequence you use them in.
4. Store items according to their function so if they do similar things store them together.

5. Eliminate multiple items that do the same thing and use a single one that does multiple functions.
6. Make storage places larger than items stored there so it is easy to remove and put them back.
7. Make storage places accessible and comfortable to use.

3rd S - Shine

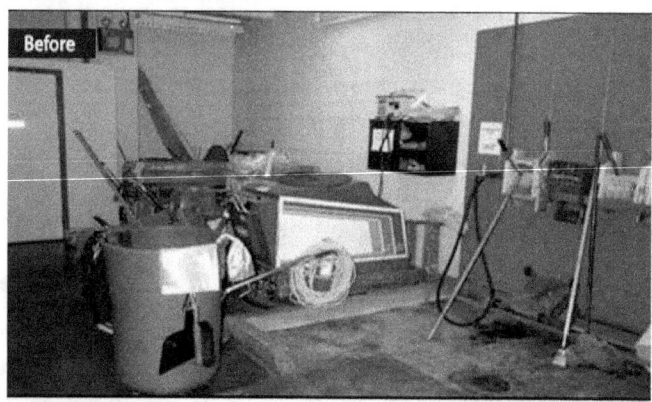

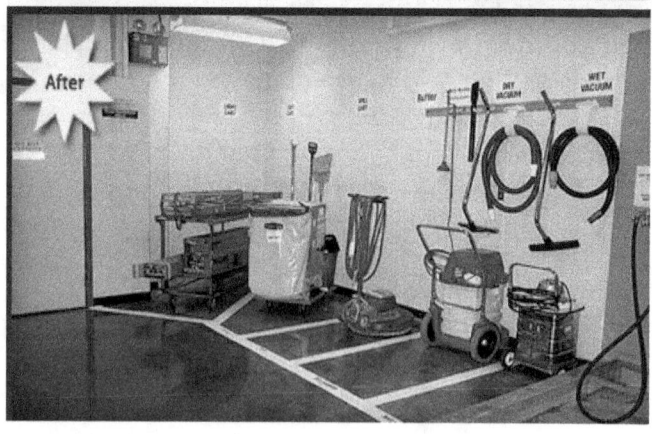

Shine (Inspect Through Cleaning)

Many people mistake 5S for a "housekeeping" program. A well 5S'd plant is clean, but not simply because it's nicer to work in a clean environment. We clean to inspect our equipment. Things like oil leaks, worn bearings, loose fasteners, etc are much easier to find when the equipment is regularly cleaned.

As someone wipes down a machine, their eye is forced to look at the machine. They therefore have a much better chance of finding something that has just gone wrong.

4th S - Standardize

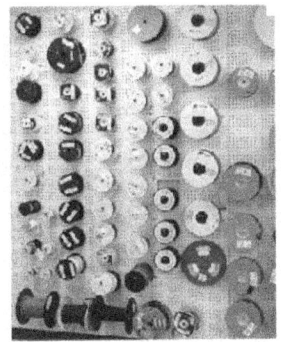

After

Easy access to all wire. Find what you want quickly. Spools take ¼ of the space to store.

Before

Shelving took up a lot of space. Correct wire was hard to find quickly. Had to move spools around to get what you were after.

Standardize

This is the heart of 5S. A process which is not performed the same way every time is out of control, and more importantly, is not improvable. Standardization requires that things be labelled, work instructions be posted, and that associates working in an area follow all follow the same standard method.

It is perfectly acceptable to change a process, but the newly changed process has to become the new standard.

5th S – Sustain

5S	TASK	TEAM
SORT		
SET-IN-ORDER		
SHINE		
STANDARDIZE		
SUSTAIN		

Sustain

The hardest of the S's. Sustain requires constant vigilance. The best way to sustain 5S is to make it a regular part of your jobs. Another excellent way is to create a metric for 5S. These metric needs to be publicly posted for all to see.

"Whatever You Measure Will Get Better"
We measure all kinds of things in our daily life. We use our speedometer to make sure we don't drive too fast on the highway. We measure the air temperature with a thermometer to know whether we should wear a jacket outside. If we want to improve something in our lives, like losing weight, we carefully weigh ourselves every week, or analyze our bowling scores to see if the new bowling ball helped like we had hoped.

One of the great truths to life is that we will tend to improve anything that we measure. We track our factory's labour utilization in order to squeeze every drop of efficiency we can get from our associates. We measure our scrap rates to ensure our corrective actions are actually reducing them.

If we are really smart, we let everybody know how we are doing on scrap rates and labour efficiency. We want allies in our fight to improve, and sharing that information helps enlist these allies on the shop floor.

What is a "Visual Metric"?

A visual metric is, at its most basic, simply a measurement that we make public. However, in order to be effective, it needs the following attributes:
1. Be publicly posted and very easy to understand.
2. Have both a "Goal" and an "Actual" value.
3. Be current (as recently as the last hour if possible).
4. Be about things the local associate can effect, but support global objectives.
5. Be easy to get (preferably without any computers!).

Similarly, there are some rules about what not to do:
1. Not include things we can't control (like stock price).
2. Not be too numerous (10 items max!).
3. Not be out of date.

Updating Methods

When we update visual metrics, we like to update them by hand by the person doing the work. We want to create an emotional sense of ownership with the person doing the work. The act of writing down a metric (especially if it is below target) will enhance this sense of ownership and responsibility. On the other hand, if they simply take a computer printout and post it on the bulletin board, that emotional sense of responsibility is greatly diminished.

This is why we say that metrics should be simple enough to gather with nothing more complex than a clipboard and a calculator.

Management Reaction

The second most important part of visual metrics is the reaction they generate in management. Management has to be seen as actively reacting to both positive and negative results on the metric. Ideally, these responses are generally positive, even when the data is poor. We encourage managers to find the root cause of the problem and correct it, rather than shooting the messenger. Most importantly, we want managers to praise accomplishments.

If management is seen to be ignoring these metrics, they actually have a negative impact on performance. If the boss doesn't seem to care how the facility is performing, why should anyone care? Be sure you are seen publicly reviewing and reacting to the data on the metric boards.

Chapter 18: Day By the Hour Boards

A "Day-by-the-Hour" board (also sometimes known as a "Pitch Board") is a special type of visual metric that clearly lays out expectations for an operation on an hourly basis, and then continuously records how well we meet those expectations. If used properly, it can have an astounding impact on productivity.

I have personally seen a Day-by-the-Hour board boost productivity by over 40%, although they typically increase productivity by a more reasonable 5% to 10%. They are especially useful for critical bottleneck operations when a product family is backordered and your customers are screaming.

A Day-by-the-Hour board has both a practical and a psychological component that combine to engage the workforce in improving productivity. It also helps us to respond quickly to problems as they develop, and gives us the opportunity to minimize the impact of routine problems.

How They Work

Managers set goals for each hour, for each day, for each work cell. These goals are posted in a public place, close to the operation.

Operators publicly record actual output every hour as they work. Everyone, including the person doing the work, can instantly see how well the operation is performing compared to the goal.

Managers publicly review and react to good/bad results. They publicly praise good results, and work to eliminate the problems which cause poor performance.

Step 1 - Goal Setting

One of the key reasons that D-b-t-H board work so well is that they force managers to set realistic goals for each operation. In many cases I have seen, a lack of a good expectation is the first of many problems preventing excellent performance. When creating a D-b-t-H board, managers have to first determine what they actually expect, and then they have to communicate that expectation to all associates in a clear and professional manner.

The goal has to be "realistic" in that it can be achieved if the operating associate follows the established procedure(s), the equipment operates as expected, and the quality of the incoming material is consistent. (Please note that this does not mean the equipment has to run all the time; it means the equipment has to operate consistently; good or bad from day to day.)

The goal also has to vary with the actual operating time in each hour. For example, if the operators are given a half-hour lunch at noon, the goal for the noon hour would be half the normal goal. Don't forget to include allowances for start-up time, end of shift cleanups, breaks, meetings, etc.

Similarly, the goal also will often change with type of product being run. Slower running products have a lower goal, and faster or easier products have a higher goal.

Beware that the goal is often different from "budget standard", as represented by the production rates loaded into the organization's computerized budget. In most places I have worked, everyone knows the "budget standard" is a convenient fiction, and that the actual expected production rate (the true standard rate) is significantly different from the budget. The D-b-t-H boards should use the actual, real standard, as defined by the manager's expectations. This means the associate is comparing their performance to the actual, realistic, and personal expectation of the manager, not to some arbitrary imposed budgetary standard. This in itself is very powerful because it means that when the output matches the goal, the production associate has met the personal objective of the manager. Likewise, if the goal is not met, the associate has let down the manager on a personal level, in addition to raising production costs by not being productive enough.

Often, you will find that managers are very reluctant to set goals, especially if they do not know what the goal should be. They hesitate to set a goal that is too loose, because then they may not get as many products as was possible. Likewise, they fear setting an unattainable goal that is too aggressive and will simply de-motivate their associates. The end result is that they set no goal, which is the worst of all possibilities. The solution to this problem is to have the manager make his best estimate of the goal. This goal does not have to be "perfect" because it will probably not be permanent. In fact, it should change as the associates get better at achieving the goal.

The manager can also simply ask the operators what a reasonable goal would be. The manager may have to allow his veneer of invincibility to crack a little, and the operators may tend to fudge the truth a bit, but this is still better than not having any goal set at all. Also, the interaction of having the associates set their own goals tends to reinforce the validity and importance of those goals. In other words, how can they miss a goal that they themselves set?

Step 2 - Record Output

The operator has to stop every hour and record his actual output. It is very important that this recording be done in a timely manner. Don't allow the operator to hold all his data until the end of the shift, as this will defeat the whole point of doing the board. He must record his output in real time every hour.

It is great to also record any comments as to why the goal was not met, or why the goal was exceeded.

The actual act of stopping and writing the data has a profound psychological impact on the entire operation. The operator has to publicly evaluate his own performance and give himself a grade. He cannot go on a "5 minute vacation" because this will be seen in the output numbers. Likewise, he can't come back late from lunches and breaks because those hours will also be short.

Nobody wants to give themselves a bad grade, so operators will naturally tend to work more diligently if they are being measured (remember "whatever you measure gets better"). Since the D-b-t-H board is posted in a very public place, this means that everyone gets to see how the operation is performing. While it is possible that peer pressure may tend to depress the output of stellar performers, my experience has been the opposite; poor performers feel the need to raise their output to the norm.

Step 3 - Management Reaction

This is the most important part of the entire system, and the part that is most likely to lead it to fail. Managers must publicly review the data several times per day. Then, they must react to the data. This reaction can be as simple as asking what went wrong during a bad hour, or praising the associate for hitting the goal during a good hour.

One major benefit from using D-b-t-H boards is that technical problems don't come as a surprise at the end of the shift. Managers check the board throughout the day, and can instantly see if some nagging, but not catastrophic problem has been interfering with production. They can then (potentially) take steps to correct those problems before they ruin the entire day's production. How many times has an operator fought some problem on a machine all shift, never wanting to "bother" the manager by asking for help? With D-b-t-H boards, they don't have to ask for help because the manager quickly sees that help is required.

In order to enhance the "public" nature of this reaction, it is good for managers to write comments on the D-b-t-H board. Typically, these are words of encouragement, while criticisms are done privately to the associate. I like to circle good hours in a red marker simply to show that I have recognized the excellent performance of the operator.

Many managers dread this part of the process because they don't want to have to acknowledge all the problems that occur. They are very busy, and are afraid that if they acknowledge a new problem, they will have to fix that problem too. However, if they never acknowledge the problem, it will never go away! Also, just acknowledging the problems caused by an unreliable machine or poor raw materials can go a long way to improving the emotional climate of the operation, and this will usually improve output by encouraging the associate. Nobody thinks the manager is a superman (except the manager, of course), so nobody will expect that every problem will be solved immediately. They do expect, however, that the manager will acknowledge the problem and begin to take steps to correct the problem.

How They Fail

Despite being a very simple process, the D-b-t-H system can actually hurt productivity if not done properly. Here are some ways that it is likely to go wrong:

Managers Don't Regularly Review the Data

This is the most common reason for failure of this system. Managers are always "too busy" to visit the board and react to the data.

If managers ignore the data, it can actually lower productivity because it undercuts the manager's professionalism and credibility in the eyes of the associate. Why should the associate spend extra time recording data when the manager does not have time to view it? And if the manager is "too busy" to view the data, it must not be very important. And if the data is unimportant, then the actual performance must not be very important either.

On the other hand, if the manager reviews the data often, and frequently praises good outcomes, or asks questions about poor production, the associate will realize how important the entire process is, and will also treat the process and the output as important.

Associates fill out the board at the end of the day

Filling out the board at the end of the day does almost nothing to improve productivity. All we have done is added an extra clerical duty to the production associate. It is the public act of giving themselves a grade which is one of the most powerful aspects of this system. Further, without this public data, no one can tell if the operation is having trouble.

If the associates don't fill out the board every hour, how come the manager has not noticed this? Since we did not catch them not filling it out, we have completely undercut our professionalism and authority.

Part 2: Why Lean Fails

Chapter 19: Can You Avoid Lean Failure?

A friend of mine asked a great question in response to one of my recent Lean books. His question was in essence how do you keep Lean initiatives moving ahead and not going the way of another flavour of the month program. We have all seen managers with the best intentions launch new initiatives that were supposed to be the wave of the future only to see them fizzle out after a few weeks or months. Lean initiatives are no different. Many organizations have tried Lean and either abandon it completely or don't take it very far. So what makes the difference between companies that tried Lean and those that are leading the pack?

A successful launch of Lean is in some respects like getting lean with one's weight. There are no quick fixes. There are no easy solutions and it takes work. You cannot make a New Year's resolution to lose weight then go back to your old habits after a few weeks or months and expect to stay Lean. It takes discipline over the long haul.

Successful Lean organizations will have several characteristics

First and foremost, organizations embarking on a Lean transformation must have someone who is passionately committed to the process and can keep others on board. According to Industry Week Magazine, 70% of all organizational change initiatives fail because there is a lack of lasting commitment. With this in mind, the higher in the organization this committed leader is the better. This Lean leader must be someone who has the authority to set direction for the long-term.

There also needs to be accountability up and down the chain of command. Lean will need to bring results if it is to survive. I doubt it will work if it's not part of everyone's annual goals and bonuses. Your company needs a way to keep Lean on the radar.

Thirdly, these organizations need to have a core group that truly thinks Lean. This group can be developed over time while on the Lean journey. Lean is a way of thinking and not just a box of tools. The journey is more than learning the tools. It is a culture change. Your organization will fall into the Lean toolbox mentality without a core group of people who can keep reminding everyone that it's a process.

Successful Lean organizations have a culture of employee engagement. This culture will need to be quickly cultivated if it is not already there. The average line operator will need to see how Lean benefits them.

Finally, there needs to be structure to facilitate and support the process.

This has certainly been an important topic in recent years and is very relevant today. You can find many references to what causes Lean to fail and what is required for success. There are many discussions in several LinkedIn groups, and books documenting successful Lean organizations. The successful organizations are the ones who are willing to invest for the long-term. Which describes your organization? Does your team keep an eye on the long-term goals even when dealing with today's issues or do they drop everything for the weekly or even daily crisis? Is your organization ready for Lean?

Chapter 20: Why Lean is Hard

If Lean is so obvious, why do so many people screw it up?

Lean Manufacturing is surprisingly simple, yet also surprisingly easy to screw up. It doesn't usually "fail" so much as never produce anything other than extra work for the participants and then die a slow death. Here is how I have seen it die.

Lack of Commitment

The whole organization has to be committed to Lean, starting at the top. Starting a Lean effort creates extra work for everyone. If the top management at a site doesn't buy into the effort, the worker-bees who actually do it will tire of the effort before the results appear. Lean doesn't necessarily have to be important to Headquarters, but the top guy on site has to be fully committed, even if the Lean effort has to become a local insurgency.

Adopting Lean is like getting religion; it has to change your whole outlook on life. The cliché about Lean not being the latest "program" is absolutely true. Since many of the benefits of Lean are difficult to objectively quantify, they have to be taken on faith (and later, experience). If the pointy-haired boss just read about Lean in the latest issue of Industry Week, and wants to try "that Lean stuff", you are doomed.

The Accountants Lie to You

Traditional standard cost systems often work against Lean. They do several bad things, including:

1. They consider inventory as an asset, while we know unsold inventory is a liability.
2. They place little emphasis on cash flow, and greatly undervalue the cost of money.
3. They completely ignore delivery cycle time.
4. They allocate fixed costs rather than considering the differential costs of business activities, etc, etc.

Good Lean accountants (yes, they do exist!) understand that "Standard Costs" are an accounting fiction which (sometimes) helps make good business decisions. Lean looks at the total waste of a business and maximizes added value. Accountants need to keep the big picture in mind.

My favourite accounting tool is the pro-forma (In the UK we call it capital justification or CAPEX).

When a major financial decision has to be made (such as a major capital expenditure), two pro-formas need to be created:

1. The business with the investment.
2. The business without the investment.

Then it is a simple matter of picking the most advantageous business result of the two pro-formas.

It Takes a Big Chunk of Work Up-Front

Implementing Lean takes a lot of work. Worse, the resulting improvements are difficult to trace to specific Lean activities. Lean requires good plant organization and planning, which takes a significant amount of time to accomplish.

When you are up to your butt in alligators, it's hard to take the time to drain the swamp. Even if you believe lowering the water will make your life easier someday, it's hard to consider drainage canals when there are teeth chomping on your leg. And if you're not convinced that lowering the water is a good idea, it's easy to forget about that canal plan for a while.

The Improvement Are Mistakes You Don't Make

Some of the biggest benefits from Lean are the mistakes that you don't make. No business plan would ever have built in allowances for these mistakes, so you never see the "gain" to the plan.

For example: Reduced Work in Process (WIP) let's you find problems faster, so when you have to re-work product, you re-work less. This saves a pile of money, but the accountants will never know it.

5S keeps your equipment cleaner and better maintained, so you find that critical loose bolt before it shuts down the machine for hours.

Procedures are generally obvious, so associates make fewer mistakes.

Cash Costs Too Little

With interest rates at historical lows, the accountants value cash too lightly. But like gasoline to the motorist stranded on the side of the road, cash can be very valuable when you don't have any.

I once worked for a company that was solidly profitable, but went bankrupt with millions of unsold inventory sitting peacefully in a warehouse. Cash is very expensive!

Often there is not one specific reason for why lean projects (or other improvement initiatives for that matter) fail. It is a combination of several. Below are listed "the usual suspects" and unfortunately their existence is more the rule, than the exception.

Initiatives do not properly involve the leaders

Local leaders; especially middle management are from the external experts' point of view often seen as people who should simply "buy-in" to the already developed and "perfect" solutions. However, even if they would agree whole-heartedly, it is never the same as if they had gotten their own hands dirty and made an active (instead of just re-active) part of the development process.

There are a lot of reasons for why it is good to involve leaders, but the primary one is, that people are simply a lot more enthusiastic about their own work rather than somebody else's. This will also get them away from fearing the changes into seeing them as a potential.

"Lean" changes are "applied" instead of integrated into the processes

For instance, putting performance measurement boards up, that are based on the existing (and flawed) KPI-structures without connection vertically (through the hierarchy) or horizontally (through the workflow). This especially happens in bigger organizations where the lean initiatives is just another task on the balanced score card: We have "performance measurements", thus we are "in green".

Too much focus on the tools

Lean has some strong tools (which are mostly (appreciatively) stolen from others), but the use of tools will fail if the foundation lacks. Proper use of tools requires an overview of where to apply them (processes) and both a will and the ability to apply them correctly (culture + lean understanding).

These conditions are rarely met satisfactorily (at least in summary). Until this happens it is better to either focus on building up these conditions or to build them up through the use of these tools (among other things).

"Pushing" motivation onto people instead of removing constraints

An inspiring speech can motivate many people, but it is soon forgotten. It is the same as when people see a fitness commercial in January and then run out to get a membership, which they never do anything seriously about. Lasting motivation needs to come naturally by removing those things that inhibits it.

This can be difficult to create within each individual, but relatively easy if one starts by focusing on the external influences. Supportive leadership, involvement and a focus on people's concerns can create very significant results and does not need expensive courses or politically problematic structural changes (these can come later).

When these constraints are removed, one will experience that motivation comes a lot more naturally, and this frees up valuable time that can be spend on what really matters; making value-adding solutions.

Too many initiatives

It is often a lot more fun to initiate something rather than actually implementing it. One of the major reasons for this is quite simply that things go wrong and reality bites. Ironically this results in a lot more projects (that is, 2 or more) than each department can handle and thus; things go a lot more wrong.

But the lean principle of flow also applies when driving change. Focus on one thing, get it right, finish it (exclude on-going re-views and continuous improvements, naturally) and then go on to the next.

Uncoordinated and too complex an approach

The organization needs to be capable of doing changes before it tries to transform itself. If this ability does not exist, then we will get even more of those un-sustained results, we are so used to. An often seen case is to make an elaborate cross-organizational project that crashes down.

Instead, start by building up the departments before trying to make the "perfect" solution in a quick "go". This is of course in contrast to the principle of not sub-optimizing, but one needs to walk before attempting to run a marathon. This building up of the departments includes creating focused leaders, efficient department-based improvement structures, motivated employees (who can see the benefits of improvement) and simplified, transparent processes.

Invalid and unreliable KPI's, data and plans are seen as infallible

Unless specific altruistic goals are given, then all decisions must be made with the purpose of increasing the company's profit from a holistic (non sub optimizing) point of view. This is rarely the case, because it is usually not in the individual person's best (short-term) interest. This makes all but the most idealistic/enthusiastic take bad decisions.

Of course, both the reliability and the validity of the KPI's needs to be improved significantly as soon as possible in order to make the good decision a rational and self-preserving one. There also needs to be a focus on transparent and well-understood processes where actual value creation is clear for everybody to see.

However, KPI's and plans are, at best, only a very rough simplification of what reality actually is. This is also the case with good KPI's and reliable data. In order to make people act as a team across the entire organization (or at least through their closest internal supplier/customer network), a holistic optimizing mentality has to develop. This development needs to start with the top management and be rolled out through the hierarchy. Then, if a subordinate leader sacrifices one KPI/plan in order to make significant improvements elsewhere, then the decision is both supported and coordinated with the supervising leader.

Lack of resources

Real change requires a real effort. However, this can also be a reason to include a focus on employee and leadership efficiency in the first initiatives. This way, there are the resources necessary and management have a better reason to ensure people, that lean does not equal firings (although firings in some cases can be necessary, it will often make the change process a lot more difficult and top-down.

Blaming people instead of systems (cultural, technical, political, organizational etc.)

Almost all of the problems in an organization are the result of the way the systems work. Although individual responsibility still exists, it solves nothing try to find someone to blame, when fixing the root cause in the system would remove the problem in the first place.

Chapter 21: When Lean Thinking Fails

For the past 20 years, I have been a big advocate of Lean Thinking. I believe when the principles are properly understood and applied, the upside for productivity improvements is nearly infinite. When you think of the various types of waste in most processes today and the possibility of cutting them in half, then half again, and half a third time, it is easy to get excited.

I have personally witnessed numerous lean thinking initiatives that have improved productivity by large amounts (like 40-60%) in short periods of time with minimal capital expenditures. The track record is well documented by numerous authors. What we hear about less often are the failed attempts and the damage that can result when the tools are misapplied or poorly used.

If you try to drive a wood screw using a hammer, the result is going to be disappointing. If you try to use a trenching machine without proper training and safety equipment, you are likely to cut off your foot. So it is with the Lean tools; one needs to have the right tool for each application and be adept at using the tool properly to enjoy the benefits. Let us explore some reasons why Lean Tools sometimes backfire and cause damage rather than providing the service they are capable of producing.

First, I will list just a few of the most popular tools and their use as a way of grounding this discussion:

Kaizen: This is a structured event (normally one week in duration) where the old process is disassembled and put back together in a new and more efficient configuration.

Process Flow Maps: These are flow charts using precise rules that allow designers to actually see what is happening with new eyes. Often, what is really happening in a process is not clear to the uneducated eye.

Kan Ban: This is a technique to reduce inventory by postponing the ordering of new parts until the last minute before it is necessary. You probably have a jar of peanut butter in your refrigerator and a spare one on the shelf. You do not need a case of 24 jars because as soon as you open the one on the shelf, you can get a replacement. Kan Ban allows this same philosophy in more complex operations.

Pull Orders: The idea here is to produce product only when there is a customer who is waiting to receive it. It is the opposite of "push" production where items are made to stock and put in inventory.

Spaghetti Diagrams: These scribble diagrams allow designers to see the walking patterns of individuals throughout a shift. By studying the patterns, it is usually possible to significantly reduce the mileage covered by an individual working the process.

The Visual Workplace: This is the concept of a place for everything and everything in its place. It also serves to de-clutter any work area.

When properly applied under the guidance of a master in Lean Principles, any team can dramatically improve productivity and quality without jeopardizing customer service. This also serves to reduce inventory and storage costs. Unfortunately, when not properly managed, these same techniques can make matters worse and cause headaches. Let's examine why this can be the case.

Lack of real management commitment

Quite often management sees the carrot dangling in front of them to reduce costs and says "go ahead and have a Kaizen." The team is not properly configured or given the time and resources to do the job right. There is no lean expert overlooking the process. The team starts out with good intentions, but eventually totally mucks up the entire process. It can be very expensive to bring the process back to where it was. In the meantime, customers may have totally run out of product.

Thinking of Lean as an activity rather than a way of life

Lean principles will apply all of the time, and continuous improvement is part of the process. If management views a lean activity as a "one off" event, the results will be suboptimal at best and disastrous at worst. A good lean application is more like learning a new religion for life and not a band aid to put on a broken process until things heal.

Trying to do too much too fast

Although most lean work involves revolutionary improvements, the application is more evolutionary. It takes an even application to keep the momentum going forward. It often means educating teams of people, which can appear to be rather expensive. When managers get greedy and try to swing for the fences each time at bat, there are going to be some strikeouts.

Failing to reinforce the culture

A good lean application means a different culture that is self sustaining. If leadership does not foster or nurture the methods by giving proper air time and reinforcement, then people will recognize this was just another flavour of the month and become sour on the ideas.

Cashing benefits by chopping off heads

Working on lean programs results in productivity gains. If these improvements do not foster growth of more sales, there are fewer people needed in the organization. If management is not careful with how the benefits of productivity are turned into cash, then the people making those improvements will sabotage the effort. I have seen several applications where a Kaizen lead to a reduced need for workers. You can imagine the chilly reception workers will give the next time a Kaizen is suggested.

These were just five of the ways Lean Thinking can backfire and not produce the sustained benefits imagined. Leaders need to apply the techniques carefully and with real commitment to enjoy the long term improvements.

Chapter 22: Why Lean Programs Fail?

Toyota's success has inspired tens of thousands of organizations to adopt some form of a lean program. The term was introduced in The Machine That Changed the World and later in Lean Thinking as a new paradigm that was as monumental as the shift from craft-style to mass production. The focus of lean is on the customer and the value stream. You can say it is a pursuit of perfection by constantly eliminating waste through problem solving. Certainly an organization that is truly dedicated to becoming lean is on a path toward excellence.

Yet a large survey we conducted in 2012 found that only 2 percent of companies that have a lean program achieved their anticipated results.

1. More recently, the Shingo Prize committee, which gives awards for excellence in lean manufacturing, went back to past winners and found that many had not sustained their progress after winning the award. The award criteria were subsequently changed.
2. Why is the pursuit of excellence through lean so difficult?

Where Does Improvement Come From?

When we look at a Toyota plant, we see many good ideas, and it appears that the company has a department of Toyota Production System (TPS) geniuses who design and implement all these lean innovations. We might ask whether these ideas are standardized and implemented in all Toyota plants in the exact same way. Are the TPS experts telling the plants what to do and auditing them to see if they are following the best practices?

The reality is that very little that you see at a Toyota site is the result of one person with a big idea that got standardized across plants. More often, what you see is today's condition, which is the result of many small steps, some of which were discarded and others embraced. It was the result of many cycles of plan-do-check-act (PDCA), and it is different throughout Toyota because different organizations are on different learning cycles.

Everybody is jumping on the Lean Bandwagon, but many are Being Taken for a Ride. Industry Week, May 1, 2008.

Robert Miller, Executive Director of the Shingo Prize, interviewed on radiolean.com, July, 2010. "About 3 years ago we felt we needed deep reflection. After 19 or 20 years we went back and did a significant study of the organizations that had received the Shingo Prize to determine which ones had sustained the level of excellence that they demonstrated at the time they were evaluated and which ones had not...We were quite surprised, even disappointed that a large percentage of those organizations that had been recognized had not been able to keep up and not been able to move forward and in fact lost ground. We studied those companies and found that a very large percentage of those we had evaluated were experts at implementing tools of lean but had not deeply embedded them into their culture."

"An antidote to this dilemma of resistance to change is to develop strong mental circuits not for solutions, but for how to develop solutions."

My colleagues, who has spent years researching how Toyota does what it does and how to better teach companies that are on a quest for excellence, summarizes what they found in the concept of the routine process for making improvements, which they suggests underlies striving to meet challenges at Toyota.

We have both concluded from our different journeys and experiences with companies that people have had a fundamental misunderstanding of what the Toyota Production System is in practice. We mistook lean solutions for the process that leads to what we see in a Toyota plant. We need to look more deeply at the human thinking and processes that underlie specific practices that we observe.

For example, early in our understanding of TPS we thought of heijunka (Production levelling, also known as production smoothing) as a powerful tool to level the workload and reduce inventory. But what we found from our experiences with companies was that establishing the heijunka pattern itself changes little in most cases. What is more important is the behaviour generated by viewing the heijunka pattern as a target condition and following the improvement process in striving to achieve it. It's the systematic, iterative

119

working through the obstacles, step-by-step, that actually improves processes, and it takes practice to acquire the skills and mindset for how to do that.

Similarly, the overt purpose of kanban is to provide a way of regulating production between two processes, so that the supplying process produces only what is needed when it is needed. The invisible purpose of kanban, which we missed, is to provide a target condition. Kanban is a predetermined pattern between a supplier and customer process that, with the right leadership and culture, is used to generate behaviour to work through the obstacles to achieve that target condition.

The difference between the visible and invisible purposes of heijunka, kanban and other lean tools is the difference between attempts at implementation of tools, and using the tools as part of deliberately practicing a routine for continuous improvement.

Learning a New Way of Thinking and Acting

Recent findings in neuropsychology demonstrate that people develop well-worn neural pathways that make it comfortable to do things the same way again and again. While humans derive a lot of their sense of security and confidence from this, the content of what we do will in fact be changing, whether intentionally or not, because conditions are always changing. An antidote to this dilemma of resistance to change is to develop strong mental circuits not for solutions, but for how to develop solutions.

The management task, then, is to have the organization's members practice a behaviour pattern, like the improvement process, that achieves this. We need a routine not just for doing the work, but for continually improving the work. That routine is missing in organizations that use top-down management objectives, so managers have no choice but to blindly start.

The improvement process is a way we can break down an abstract vision into a series of descriptive target conditions, and through striving to achieve them both develop and utilize the creative powers of people. It involves teaching people a standardized, conscious means of grasping the essence of situations and responding scientifically by working iteratively.

The improvement process is a routine to teach and learn that mobilizes people's capability to achieve desired conditions. The improvement process is a way to achieve things that you don't know how you are going to achieve.

Toyota's improvement process has been taught implicitly in some parts of Toyota for decades. The TPS mentor would do this by giving the student a challenge, such as to make a breakthrough in performance in a process (e.g., combine these two production cells into one mixed model cell that operates on two shifts with four people and can respond to changes in customer demand). Even if the mentor has a notion of how the challenge might be achieved, he does not share it with the student. His task is to lead the student into developing good habits for working through problems, via intensive questioning-based coaching on this problem.

We missed this underlying skill and mindset development focus of TPS. For example, in an organization we observed the Chief Operating Officer decided to hold plant managers accountable for running a certain number kaizen events to achieve a certain level of productivity improvement. It became slash-and-burn lean with no sustainability and no continuous improvement, i.e., old school, outcome focused, carrot and stick motivation.

These days there is more structure to Toyota's coaching process, but the relationship between mentor and student is at the core of how Toyota gets improvement to be a deeply embedded routine. To have enough coaches they are often the direct managers of the students, but the managers can always use training too and should themselves have a coach from inside or outside the organization.

There seems to be a strong belief in Western business that you select people with good innate work/management characteristics (habits), and then you give them outcome targets. In contrast, Toyota selects people for their openness to learning, and then develops the desired work/management characteristics (habits) through practice after they hire in. Neuroscience is showing us that the adult human brain is more plastic than we believed, and that's what Toyota is taking advantage of in order to develop a deliberate culture.

Challenge Demands Learning

Research has repeatedly shown that when a task is relatively easy i.e., when the path to the target condition is pretty clear then managing by results and with extrinsic motivators can work well enough. The task is basically to get it done, and the organization's leaders need not overly concern themselves with ensuring that people are employing a systematic, scientific approach to achieving the target condition.

On the other hand, if the task is a challenge i.e., the path to the target condition is unclear and has to be discovered via iterative learning then managing by results and extrinsic carrot and stick motivators does not compete so well. In that case, how people go about striving for their target conditions becomes important, and, in competitive markets, is something with which leaders will need to concern themselves.

When we look at lean in this way it is not only a set of techniques for eliminating waste, but a process by which managers as leaders develop people so that desired results can be achieved, again and again. That means coaching people in practicing an improvement process every day.

So Why Lean Fails?

Don't ever implement without the understanding, preparation, commitment, measurement, and strategy involved in how to do it. If you begin to try and go down that path of lean, without a good strategy and those other factors in place, you are pretty much going to fail at some point in time, it's going to probably fail, and that's one thing we want to avoid.

There are eight key elements to implementing lean successfully, but if you fail to execute these elements properly in one or more areas, you will have limited to no success. The very first commitment that will define your success or failure is taking a major leap of faith. If you're not willing to make that leap of faith, don't even try. Eliminating waste will be the second obstacle you face, primarily because one of the greatest obstacles western managers face is in understanding the difference between eliminating and only minimizing.

What about our great quest for the magic button, that a new tool will make all of our problems disappear, and our misconception that lean is going to be like that magic button. We assured that, "Yes, Kaizen/lean has lots of tools, they have many options to be used, but kaizen and lean is much more than that. There are no magic buttons, and if you continually go to look for those magic buttons you are going to be very inefficient and disappointed. You are going to try one thing, and then you are going to try another, and then another without actually successfully implementing the process.

Leadership, commitment, understanding, timing, preparation, strategy, measurement and communication with the combination of teamwork are the eight key factors to achieving success in lean. As a leader you have to support the changes 100 percent. If you have any doubt in the process with regard to your commitment, you have a very slim chance of success and improvement. More importantly, it is your responsibility to lead the change and include your employees in the entire process. The biggest untapped resources you have for improvement are your employees.

Some of the best ideas come from the people that are doing the work. They are the ones that do it every day, and they are the ones that are going to provide you with your best suggestions.

You can know a lot about something but not really understand it. One of the biggest mistakes about trying to improve quality is trying to improve quality in the product itself. That is the wrong approach. You don't ever try to fix quality by analyzing the product only. You have to go and fix the process you use to make the product or complete the service, and as you improve that process your quality improves.

Without proper preparation it leads to failure, without commitment it leads to failure, without an understanding of what it's supposed to accomplish it leads to failure, and without leadership it's going to lead to failure.

Allowing a suitable amount of time needed to be properly prepared is a common mistake. If you rush into 5S, you are just doing a spring cleaning. You have to not only learn as the leader, but you are going to have to learn to teach the people that are involved in your staff and your organization in regards to it.

Over and over again, people fall back into old habits shortly after they implement a few quick improvements. Success is often missed due to poor timing.

You will make the most progress simply by starting with small steps and by continuing to build on them. It's also important to keep track of your progress because without measurement everything's debatable. You need the data.

The last topics to be touched on in this chapter were communication and teamwork. Both elements are vital to maintaining a well oiled machine. Communication is very often one way, very often a situation in which we think we are communicating well, we think we are getting that information out, but there is no communication unless both parties understand it.

Many things can go wrong in this step so it is important to communicate often, and communicate effectively. Ask questions; make sure everyone is on the same page and working together as a team. The approach of teamwork is the key difference between failure and success. Without teamwork, you will fail at lean. Teamwork allows you to achieve results you would never be able to achieve individually.

If you are able to recognize and avoid these common mistakes we touched on when implementing lean in your organisation, you will find more success in eliminating the waste and improving your productivity.

Chapter 23: Why Lean Fail in Some Industries

Change does not come easily for most industries. There are a wide variety of reasons why people, companies, and industries do not embrace change. Without a willingness to change, companies get stuck in patterns that prevent them from not only progressing operationally, but also culturally.

That Great Lean Expansion

In recent years, lean manufacturing has gained favour in the many industries. Viewed as a means of cutting waste and subsequent costs, lean is perceived as a way to recover income by improving operational efficiencies.

We see numerous lean initiatives being introduced in the industries.

1. 5S, a process for systematizing workplace organization, has seen widespread implementation across the industries among those who have adopted lean principles. Many companies see 5S as a tool to improve process efficiency by placing tools and supplies at the point of use, and using visual management techniques to monitor processes and replenish supplies.

2. Another lean tool that has seen widespread use is the Kaizen event. These focused

process improvement activities use teams to infuse rapid, intensive, and focused attention into improving a work process over a period of only a few days. These events jumpstart lean initiatives by placing significant energy behind improvement efforts using a team approach.

3. Continued focus on quick changeovers remains a central theme. Rapid make ready techniques are viewed as a means to move non-chargeable time to chargeable time. SMED (Single Minute Exchange of Dies) improvements are achieved through substantial equipment re-engineering, as well as focusing on external processes to improve offline changeover times. We are encouraged that many equipment manufacturers are putting substantial energy into reducing make ready times, as well as standardizing the changeover process.

4. Just-in-time delivery has been around for a few years, but some companies are beginning to understand how to level and predict the flow of materials, as well as use kan-ban systems to initiate replenishment. This is particularly powerful for those companies who have successfully developed highly integrated supplier partnerships.

We are encouraged that a few companies see lean as more than just a set of tools. These companies understand the real power of lean manufacturing; the empowerment of employees to initiate systemic operational change. These companies see lean as something that goes beyond simply making incremental improvements to the bottom line.

Lean Failings

Despite a few discrete lean success stories, we are confident that lean has largely failed in companies in the western world. That is tragic. It is clear that most see lean as a set of tools to improve efficiencies. However, lean is much more than a set of tools. Its heartbeat lies in the foundational principles that underlie those tools. Remember, lean was not developed as a program for consultants to sell. Rather, lean is a realistic, logical, and proven response to fundamental business challenges. It is based on the premise that people, when challenged, informed, and properly rewarded, develop innovative solutions and drive needed business change.

Change Management Issues

So, lean isn't working in the printing industry and you should do something about it. The primary reasons lean fails focuses around five issues about change management. Review the list below and see how many of these apply to you or your business.

1. Fear of becoming something you know nothing, or little, about. Intuitively, we know that change requires becoming, or doing, something differently than we presently are. This logically breeds a certain amount of uncertainty, which most people would prefer to

avoid. We default to those things we feel we know or have greater certainty of occurring. It is far simpler to continue on a present, known course than to deviate; even when we know the current course will not likely lead us to success.

Industry articles, conferences, and consultants continually press the printing industry to become something more than "just printers." It may be intuitively easy to accept this as a concept, but it requires great courage to actually head down a different pathway for potential success, especially when short-term profits are sacrificed for sustained gains.

2. Fear of losing your identity. This applies to both companies and individuals. People, and companies, become known for something. Contemplating a new direction disrupts our fundamental beliefs about ourselves; what we stand for and what we believe in. Most change management practices dictate that managers act differently. Conceptually, this is easy to embrace, but for those involved with the required change, it attacks the core of their belief systems involving who they are and what they do. Much is written about getting rid of those who "aren't along for the ride" or "can't embrace the new thinking," but little is done to find ways to allow those who struggle with the change process to find the means to succeed. Some lean concepts require fundamental change a frightening proposition.

3. Fear surrounding the scope of what needs to be done. Many firms are not positioned for long-term

success where they stand today. Transforming a company, including the culture, is a massive undertaking for anyone; even those adept at managing change. Change must be managed concurrently with managing the existing business and may require a phased approach to reduce the feeling of being overwhelmed. Fundamental change is required while circumstances seemingly allow only incremental steps. The sheer magnitude of what needs to be accomplished stops many companies in their tracks from undertaking needed action. Transforming a company into a lean enterprise is a marathon, not a sprint.

4. Fear of moving away from existing support base. Whatever you are doing today, you got there with customer, supplier, and employee support. Your business model and methods evolved from the perceived needs of their time. The values your firm embraces have evolved from the rich history people associate with it. It is disruptive to think about altering business methodology and potentially alienating the support base your business has worked hard to earn.

5. Habits are habits because we perpetuate them. Fundamental change in a business requires change across the entire business. Yet, most businesses are organized around functions or departments that compartmentalize an employee's view, making it difficult to address business-wide needs. We have trained and rewarded people to focus on narrow segments of a business, which compounds any effort to suddenly view and act on the big picture of how

the business should operate. Lean requires both a change of habits and a change from micro to macro attention.

Much is being written regarding lean manufacturing and the rethinking of your business in lean terms. Fundamental tenets of lean include focusing on value creation as defined by your customer needs, not on the basis of what your capabilities are. Lean tools are taught at conferences and seminars to help printers identify waste and drive it out of their business. Waste is redefined from traditional paradigms around spoilage. We are taught that inventory is an asset in your financial records, is actually a form of waste and its existence leads to poor process thinking internally and also perpetuates poor financial performance.

Learning about and utilizing the various tools of lean will certainly aid improvement in a firm's cost performance. If results are tangible, and visible enough, many companies will continue to develop their expertise in lean methodology. This is the state many printers find themselves in today one of cautiously exploring lean thinking while continuing to run their business in the manner they have grown accustomed to for all the reasons written about above.

Chapter 24: Doing Lean Versus Being Lean

We feel strongly there is a substantial difference between "doing lean" and "being lean." Far too many companies are falling into the trap of "doing lean" while not undertaking the necessary changes to actually "be lean." Undertaking process improvements using only lean tools runs the risk of following so many other improvement efforts that have fizzled into oblivion after a few years of concerted effort in the industries.

Fundamental improvement requires fundamental change, and this must take place across the entire organization. Companies must be able to address the change management issues listed in previous chapter of the book and ingrain lean thinking into the core culture of their business model. Companies interested in remaining competitive, and thriving in the future, will embrace lean fully, not merely implementing select tools of convenience.

Lean works, lean is not easy, and lean is necessary for company's long-term viability.

What is your firm doing about it?

Lean efforts are aplenty. Rare are successful ones characterized by sufficient improvement in the ability to create great value by delighting customers with best in class products and services, offered reliably and responsively to change, done affordably and profitably. Nearly unheard of are sustainable successes characterized by success over years and waves of market change and leadership succession.

Why?

The few world-class organizations that compete well on 'operational excellence,' reflected in quality, variety, time to market, affordability, agility, and many other positive attributes manage the complex operating systems on which they depend based on few principles, adherence to which allows short term reliability and 'high velocity' sustained, broad based improvement and innovation. Furthermore and because of this, operations the design, running, and improvement of the complex systems for development, design, and delivery is treated as a strategic concern, occupying the time and attention of senior leaders, generation to generation.

First operational excellence is defined as a vocational craft; the skilled application of tools onto problems rather than as a principle-based profession. Then, because operational excellence is treated as a vocation, experts in standard work, line side stores and supermarkets, kanban control of just in time, and the like get relegated in role with the other skilled trades important in supportive roles and called on episodically when needed, like plumbers, electricians, radiology techs, and phlebotomists, but not core to the competitive efforts of the organization.

134

What is the solution?

First, recognize that all professional disciplines those that rise to prominence in organizations are built on simple, sound principles, and expertise is displayed by the application of those principles to ever more sophisticated situations in order to create value. Professionals use tools but are not defined by them.

Finance, for instance, is built on net present value, option pricing, and portfolio theory. Those three ideas are what are applied to the design of transactions to maximize monetary value.

Mechanical engineering is built on Newtonian mechanics, a few laws of thermodynamics, some material science. These are applied iteratively to the design of technical systems of incredible complexity, to maximize their functional value.

Strategy is built on the simple principles of positioning more strongly than weakly, vis-à-vis competitors and customers to maximize ability to capture value with products and services in markets.

Second, reframe operational excellence to be like other professional disciplines, moving from the vocational application of tools, artefacts, and isolated applications and moving to bona fide principles of design, operation, and improvement in pursuit of maximizing created value (not merely eliminating waste).

The essence of operational excellence is not (and cannot be) tools like, continuous flow, focused factories within factories, value streams, and standard work.

Rather, those tools all reflect the principle that declaring in advance of use how a system is expected to operate maximizes value by maximizing the chance to be successful by harnessing best known approaches.

Likewise, the essence of operational excellence is not poke yoke, or lines painted on the floor. Rather, those tools all reflect the principle that testing in use how a system is actually operating maximizes value by maximizing the chance of seeing problems when and where they occur.

DMAIC (Define, Measure, Analyze, Improve, Control), PDCA (plan–do–check–act or plan–do–check–adjust), and Shewhart are not 'essential' to operational excellence. All are tools reflecting the principle that solving problems with the scientific method as a bona fide hypothesis-testing exercise maximizes value by maximizing the chance of building new, useful knowledge where ignorance prevailed previously.

In short, sustainable success is impossible so long as operational excellence is explained and practiced in a tool kit approach. That allows only imitative excellence in situations imitative of the situations in which the tools were seen used. It relegates operations experts to supportive rather than organizationally leading roles.

True sustained excellence comes about from having systematic approaches for designing complex work to capture known knowledge and to see problems as they occur, to solve problems to build new knowledge, and to incorporate systemically what was learned locally. Leadership models and cultivates these skills relentlessly.

Toyota, Apple the Navy's 'nucs' program and very few others demonstrate this in their unique capacity for reliability and high velocity improvement and innovation. The corollary is proven by the near uniqueness of Toyota, Apple, and the Navy's 'nucs' program despite the near universality of lean and six sigma tools trades people and kaizen jockeys.

Chapter 25: Why Companies Fail to Achieve Lean Success

During both prosperous and difficult times, successful businesses naturally look for new ways to improve performance. However, in recent years, as the world economy suffered through one of the worst recessions in history, many companies turned in droves to Lean and other variations of continuous improvement programs to rescue their sagging businesses. But, did they really learn during this process?

Despite the enormous popularity of Lean, the track record for successful implementation of the methodology is spotty at best. Some recent studies say that failure rates for Lean programs range between 50 percent and 95 percent. To analyze this level of performance from a Lean, problem-solving perspective, continuous improvement experts should be asking. Why do so many companies fail to achieve Lean success?

While the causes are numerous and extensive, I will focus on one of the most significant reasons: failure to understand the theories and concepts of Lean and their relationship to the entire business.

What is in a Name?

First of all, there is the name itself. The commonly used term Lean manufacturing perhaps could be the worst-coined phrase for this type of continuous improvement methodology. It automatically emphasizes two things that conjure limited expectations of the functionality of this business methodology. Lean and manufacturing.

The dictionary definition of the word lean (lacking in richness, fullness, quantity; poor) brings up unfortunate connotations. When mentioned in business circles, Lean is often associated with trimming down, reducing or (most notably during the Great Recession) lack of sales or work. Thus, when the word Lean is spoken, most people immediately think of doing more work with fewer people. Because no one prefers unemployment to a stable job, figurative walls are automatically erected to defend against the inevitable layoff.

Companies considering Lean also need to understand that manufacturing is a woefully inaccurate term to describe the full uses of Lean concepts. Lean is a business methodology, not simply a manufacturing tool. It requires complete and total commitment from the highest executive levels and must cascade down to all departments and throughout all levels of business.

Lean does involve manufacturing, of course, but it also directly affects sales, customer service, human resources, research and design, finance, administration, purchasing, scheduling and building maintenance. Failure to understand how improvements (or lack thereof) made in one area will affect another can result in transformation failure. If your manufacturing team improves processing time from five days to one day, but your "pre-production" team still requires 25 days to get the order to manufacturing, you haven't gained much on the competition.

'Flavour of the Month' Resistance

Given that so many companies have misused the Lean approach, resistance is to be expected. This push-back also creates barriers to the change that needs to take place for an effective Lean transformation. Meanwhile, the understandably sceptical staff considers the methodology to be just another flavour-of-the- month that will eventually be abandoned.

But how does a Lean transformation become another flavour of the month?

Businesses in all sectors are jumping on Lean. Some truly do the research and understand what they are getting into usually realizing it is far more than they had foreseen. However, far too many believe that simply applying the tools (5S, Kaizen, value stream mapping and so on) will get them on the road to quick success. They do not take the time to learn of the theories and concepts needed to sustain the transformation. They do not review those theories and concepts thoroughly and align the business to the methodology.

Here lies an additional level of cause. As flavour-of-the-month management is so readily displayed in business today, the faith required for a Lean transformation often does not exist. Too many businesses initiate change, only to fall away when they cannot overcome this barrier.

Arguably, there are several solutions to this lack of faith in Lean. For instance, businesses committing to Lean transformation should not use the time benefits gained from Lean as an excuse to pile more work onto their employees. Simply adding more work to the pile only lowers productivity, morale, and both the physical and mental health of the staff. Taking the time to work with the employee, learning to identify necessary tasks, removing unnecessary work and discovering more available time to do more valuable work (without increasing the overall workload) will result in better understanding between employee and manager, more trust, communication, and overall employee performance.

Nor can a business use Lean as a tool for headcount reduction. Certainly, layoffs made headlines across the globe during the Great Recession, including some companies touting Lean. Many companies used the downturn in business as the excuse for layoffs, claiming they were not Lean-related, but that is like claiming it is not your fault the house burned down while holding the empty gas can and the matches.

Total Commitment

The single most significant key to a Lean implementation is that all parts of the business must make the transformation through total commitment to Lean theories, concepts and tools. For example, if your finance team is still using standard cost accounting, you will not see the financial gain of implementing Lean. If finance has no desire to change, the executive level must step in and drive change.

When Lean is implemented to reduce staff sizes or add work without eliminating waste, or is focused too heavily on manufacturing, the transformation is bound to fail. Some improvements will be made, but they will be neither sustainable nor, more importantly, continuously improved upon.

Newtonian laws state that every action has an equal and opposite reaction it is a simple theory. The difficulty lies in understanding the reaction, preparing for the reaction and working with the reaction. Failure to understand the relationship that a Lean transformation has with the entire business will cause an unexpected, and unwanted, result. We therefore concluded from our different journeys and experiences with companies that people have had a fundamental misunderstanding of what the Toyota Production System is in practice.

Part 3: Lean Failure Prevention

Chapter 26: Avoiding Lean Manufacturing Failure

If you are not careful with lean manufacturing, meaning you do not implement it correctly or use it in the correct way, you have a high chance of failing. If your company fails with lean manufacturing you actually increase, your chances of having your company fail. The reason that your company can fail if you fail with lean manufacturing is that lean manufacturing is a system that you are putting into place to help improve your manufacturing so that you can keep your customers happy. With lean manufacturing, you are going to be focusing on ways to reduce costs, which will be done by getting rid of anything that does not add value to your manufacturing process. If you do not get rid of the waste in your manufacturing plant you will end up losing money, which can led to the failure of your business because you can lose all of your customers.

One of the most common ways that people fail with lean manufacturing is not being prepared, so to avoid lean manufacturing failure you will need to make sure that you are prepared to implement lean manufacturing. You cannot expect lean manufacturing to be implemented overnight, so if you are serious about implementing lean manufacturing you will need to put forth the time and effort required to make the switch. To do this you will need to figure out ahead of the time the costs that are going to be associated with converting to lean manufacturing, you will also need to determine if you need to purchase anything to make the conversion.

Something else that you will need to do is make sure that you get the right kind of training for lean manufacturing. To ensure that you do not get the wrong kind of training for lean manufacturing you will want to do some basic research on the companies that offer lean manufacturing training, so that you can choose the instructors for your training that will best meet your needs. When interviewing instructors you want to find out about what kind of tools that they plan to use to teach you about lean manufacturing, how they recommend implementing lean manufacturing, and anything else that could possibly affect the training that they are providing.

Downtime is an important part of lean manufacturing, so you will need to make sure that you implement it correctly. Implementing down time does not mean allowing your employees to sit and talk during slow periods, if this happens your company is actually losing money. What you need to do is implement a process that your employees can follow during downtime because with any kind of manufacturing work there is going to be down time, whether the machines need to get moved or the machine breaks down. If you are experiencing down time whether scheduled or not you will need to make sure that, there is other work for your employees to do. For example, if a machine shuts down unexpectedly your employees should take advantage of that down time to clean up their work area. You can also have them clean up their work areas when there is scheduled maintenance on machines. Scheduling downtime can help prevent the unscheduled downtime that causes your company to lose money.

The last thing you need to be aware of with lean manufacturing failure is your employees failing you. This usually happens when your employees are not giving you 100%. To avoid this kind of failure you will want to do everything that you can to keep your employees happy and motivated because the happier your employees are the more productive they will be. One way to keep your employees motivated and happy is to offer them rewards for the hard work they are doing. The rewards can be raises or bonuses for achieving certain goals.

Although the goals don't have to be "perfect", they do have to be "reasonable". Establishing a goal that the associate feels is impossible will demoralize him. Why should he break his back trying to hit something he knows he can't achieve? On the other hand, a goal that is too loose risks letting the associate work less hard than they should.

The solution is to be honest when setting goals. The manager should admit that the goal is a reference, and that it may very well change once he gains more experience. (Ouch! Did you feel manager's armour chink?) Therefore, the production goal is not set in stone. It is possible (and in fact desirable) to adjust the goals after monitoring actual output over time.

Chapter 27: How to Prevent Lean Failure

The only real failure in life is the failure to try...

Although the above is true with life, with Lean there are some things that can help you avoid failure.

We have been made aware of many businesses over the last few years and witnessed in our early days as employees of large companies, struggling with Lean transformations; this has allowed us to understand how to avoid failing and for ourselves that failing was part of the learning process. However we don't want you to fail, we want you to use our experience to deliver a lean transformation effectively and successfully, where you are the enablers to your achievement of your goals.

Four things you can do to help prevent failure

1. Compelling need to change: For most change to be successful and for people to buy into it, there needs to be a reason to change. I have seen these been created by management rather than waiting until something is serious enough to necessitate change. So to prevent the "why do we need to change?" question being asked. Have a think about the "What is in it for me" for individuals at each level, if things change how will it help them? And develop a need to change if there isn't one

already in this economically challenging environment.

2. Senior leadership commitment and role modelling required behaviours: If you are in a senior position, you need to change too. The shop floor or the office or the workshops are generally a mirror of the effectiveness of the manager. If you think the office/warehouse etc can improve then so can you. To introduce Lean and other Continuous Improvement methodologies successfully generally require managers to Go and See the work taking place, to fix problems where they occur rather than from behind a desk etc.

You definitely need to practise what you preach mentality a one off is not good enough it needs to be consistent and the behaviours repeated at all levels.

"We are what we repeatedly do. Excellence then is not an act, but a habit."

3. Engagement of the people doing the work: It is commonly known that the people who know most about a process are the ones who do it each day. So why are they not utilised more to be empowered to make the changes, this may require workshops with representatives from each step of the Value Stream. Engage the people who work the process, empower them to develop their improved standards and working practices

and create a mechanism to enable them to continuously improve.

4. Standardise the principles and not necessarily the tools: A lot of consultancies have developed successful lean approaches however they are not always transferable to each team in each company they engage with therefore;

Before taking an off the shelf solution and letting consultants "do to" you. Understand fully the principles behind Lean and Continuous Improvement.

Chapter 28: How to Make Lean Succeed

The great business breakthrough of the 20th Century may be Lean (and Six Sigma) techniques that cut waste and can dramatically boost productivity. Yet many firms can't make Lean work for them.

The big challenge for any company is "the ability to make things stick" to be able to agree as a group to do things a new way, and then follow through and actually do it in that new way, consistently.

The biggest enemy of Lean is Culture specifically; Lean will fail if you attempt to introduce it into a hostile culture that resists change.

Recent MIT studies show that up to 70% of firms that institute Lean or Six Sigma don't sustain the improvements. In five years, they are back where they started.

The solution is to implement three things:
1. Vision
2. Change Management
3. Culture Change

Vision provides the "why" that motivates action.

For change management, there must be strong vision at the top and leadership to require and remind and reinforce the new way of doing things.

In the weak firm, there are change meetings that generate brief excitement, and then people leave the meeting and go back to the real world.

Culture change can occur when senior leaders recruit middle managers to champion the change. Each middle manager needs to own their own vision. That will identify the 3 or 4 things that their workgroup needs to focus on to make the change really stick.

For example, I was working with a $60 million wholesale distributor where nobody owned the inventory process. The branch managers were constantly frustrated because their client projects were always ham-strung by a lack of available inventory.

So I worked with them to create a task force of VPs plus three branch managers, reporting to and sponsored by the senior executives (CEO, CFO, an Executive VP and the company owner), who are also on this task force and who all show up for all the meetings. They read their vision statement out loud at the start of every meeting. This keeps them focused on the vision and their role in making it happen. That vision includes metrics that will measure the change.

These task force members then drive sub-task-forces to take on subsets of the vision. These sub-task-forces also have metrics that define their focus areas and measure their success and progress.

All meetings use best practice disciplines:
1. Meetings start on time.
2. Meetings end on time.

3. Teams use the meetings to make decisions.
4. Teams publish minutes from each meeting.
5. In those minutes, people get clear assignments.
6. People are held accountable by their peers for following through.

This approach has been very powerful. Within just four months, my client has completely implemented their distribution centre a keystone to the new strategy.

It was crucial that the owner started with a clear vision for customer service, and the entire project was built around that vision.

Mistakes and Safety

In the best companies, it's always safe to make a mistake, as long as you own the mistake and learn from it. Leadership needs to create that safety while requiring the learning; neither will happen on their own.

Metrics and Accountability

To maintain focus and accountability, I helped this client take the vision (which mentions four key metrics) and turn it into a dashboard. For them, the four "big dials" on the dashboard come straight out of the vision statement.
1. Revenue
2. Profit Margin
3. Inventory Turns

4. Obsolete Inventory

Other important metrics are also shown as "smaller dials" this functions in a way that is similar to a Balanced Scorecard.

Metrics tell people what they should pay attention to. People become ineffective when they aren't sure what to focus on the metrics clarify priorities.

And when the metrics reflect the vision, they become mutually reinforcing.

Blaming

But what do you do when people prefer to blame rather than change? You can set up a metric, and people will sit there, watch the metric not change, and then blame and finger-point.

Now what?

The third leg of the Culture of Action is to replace "problem solving" (which implies you screwed up, and just takes you back to your prior level) with an innovation oriented culture of "continuous improvement" (which carries no stigma and makes things permanently better).

By allowing every worker to contribute to the continuous improvement, you are taking workers who might otherwise feel like robots, and you are turning them into programmers they each day run a program they helped write, and they can feel the power that comes with making permanent changes and improvements.

I advocate using the classic PDCA (Plan-Do-Check-Act) cycle, starting not with an assumption that the current state is "broken" but rather starting with a desired future better state.

The team then compares the future state with the current state, finding the gap between the two, and brainstorms ways to close the gap. This creates the Plan.

The team then tries to do the plan. Then they check to see how it worked. Finally they Act as a group to refine and revise the Plan based on what they learned when they Checked. Then they take the revised Plan and Do it again.

I say, "Once you have change management with leadership and vision, and you have continuous improvement where you are creating a better future state, you really can build it into the culture; the habits and values; and create a true Culture of Action."

Chapter 29: Gemba Walks

Most good managers tend to spend a large part of their day on the shop floor. They are out where the work is done (the "gemba" in Japanese parlance), seeing with their own eyes the problems that occur, listening to associates, and giving advice and direction to the team. The Gemba Walk process formalizes this on-the-floor time, and combines it with Visual Metrics to create a very powerful force that fosters continual improvement and alignment of objectives.

A Gemba walk is a daily, scheduled time where the manager in a facility is out in the shop floor and publicly reviews the shop's performance as displayed on the Visual Metric boards. The manager walks through the shop, stopping at each Visual Metric board to review the current results. A lower-level manager (or better yet, an hourly associate) presents the data to the manager, who can then praise good performance and ask questions about problems which prevented good performance. The manager can also give direction and suggestions to the operating associates.

The Gemba Walk is a very quick process. The total time spent at any one Visual Metric board should not exceed 10 to 15 minutes. If there are issues that need more discussion and review, then other, more traditional systems such as production meetings should still be used for them.

Gemba Walks are often done in a "layered" manner. At the lowest layer, the Department Manager does a daily walk, and an hourly associate presents the data. At these daily walks, it is common for the local maintenance mechanics, engineers, and QC technicians to participate.

As the results are being reviewed and discussed, maintenance and engineering associates can discuss their plans to provide resolutions for technical problems. Obviously, you can't have a full-blown production meeting on the floor, but you can usually solve many simple problems that otherwise would take numerous emails or meetings to resolve.

Moving up a layer, the Site-wide Operations Manager may do a weekly walk, visiting the same Visual Metric Boards, but in this case, the Department Manager (along with his staff) will present the information. Just like the daily Gemba Walk, the senior manager provides praise and guidance, only in this case he gives that praise primarily to the Department Manager and his staff.

On these higher level walks, it often appropriate to include representatives from HR, Project Engineering, New Product Development, and Sales and Marketing. Finally, at the highest layer, the Divisional Vice President follows the same Gemba Walk process when he is on site during routine monthly visits. (For the highest layer Gemba Walk, the best practice is to have the lowest level hourly associate directly present to the highest level Vice President. The positive emotional impacts of having an hourly associate explain performance and issues to the CEO or VP cannot be overstated.)

In all cases, these reviews are done publicly. Everybody sees that the operation is measured by a clear set of metrics, and that all levels of management are interested in the results of those measures. Also, anyone may ask a question or offer information. The only caveat is that the total time at any one Visual Metric station should not exceed 15 minutes. No matter who is present, a Gemba Walk is not meant to be an all-day affair.

What a Gemba Walk is NOT

A Gemba Walk does not replace the normal Production Meeting, although it may be able to replace a large portion of it. A Gemba Walk is a great place to solve small problems, but major issues that require discussion and evaluation of detailed data will still best be served by having a traditional meeting.

A Gemba Walk is also not the time to harshly criticize a manager. We prefer the Gemba Walk to be a positive event, so constructive criticisms directed at an individual are usually best done in private. (This doesn't mean that we can't offer constructive criticism in the Gemba Walk, just that we always want to protect the egos of all the participants.)

The Benefits a Gemba Walk

Gemba Walks benefit an organization in two fundamental ways. One of them is practical, the other purely psychological. These are:

1. They allow managers to quickly identify problems on floor, and help to very quickly solve the myriad of small problems that plague all operations.
2. They foster alignment of goals by demonstrating the importance of the metrics to all the associates.

The Psychological Benefits a Gemba Walk

Let's talk psychology for a moment, and then we will spend more time delving into the practical benefits of the Gemba Walk process.

One of the critical aspects of a proper Gemba Walk is that the reviews are done very publicly. All the associates see the managers walking the shop floor. The managers are therefore available to all the associates to be able to answer questions, share concerns, or simply say hello. The associates also see that the manager truly cares about the metrics presented on the Visual Metric boards. The numbers therefore are not some abstract measure created by distant accountants; they are critical measures of how well the operation is performing. By publicly demonstrating his interest in these results, the manager is implicitly demonstrating that they are important.

Many companies struggle with keeping all of their associates (hourly and managerial) focused on the same common objectives. There are elaborate procedures (often known by the Japanese phrase "Hoshin Kanri" or the just as obtusely named "Policy Function Deployment") that are used to establish this commonality. The Gemba Walk process can almost automatically create this uniformity simply by having the managers publicly review and respond to the data on a Visual Metric Board. (Of course, it goes without saying that the Visual Metric Board must be measuring things the overall organization feels is important to achieving its objectives.)

The Practical Benefits a Gemba Walk

The Gemba Walk process has many practical benefits. We will go into detail about each one, but first let's summarize them. The benefits are:

1. They force the manager out of his office, away from his email, and out to the shop where the real action (the "gemba") is. The manager will see problems with his own eyes, hear about problems directly from the operating associates, and can take immediate action to help correct them.

2. They bring together the critical players in a shop (operators, managers, maintenance, engineers, etc) so that it is easier to take quick actions to solve small, but nagging, problems. Each person hears the same description of the problems, and each can immediately offer their expertise to help resolve them. The speed with which problems can be resolved

165

can be dramatically increased compared to traditional problem solving.

3. They help ensure the metrics used to evaluate the operation are correctly aligned with the measures used to evaluate the entire operation.

Let's discuss each of these in more detail.

Benefit: Get the Manager Out on the Floor

Every manager will tell you that he spends almost 100% of his time on the shop floor except for the time needed for phone calls, meetings, email, meetings to plan future meetings, emails to discuss and prepare for upcoming meetings, and meetings to discuss emails that were written as a result of meetings, etc, etc.

In reality, managers find that there is a giant black hole pulling them away from the shop floor and into their offices. They are chained to their computers by email!

How often have you heard someone joking about a Plant Manager that can't find the Milling Department because he's never been on the floor? (It's a common complaint, but the joke is not very funny.)

Personal Anecdote: As Operations Director, I used to get over 100 emails per day. I estimate that I spent an average of 2 minutes per email just to read them. That meant that over 3 hours per day was spent simply reading those emails. Of course, many of these emails would require investigation, planning, and thoughtful replies. No wonder a Plant Manger has to work so many hours!

Also, this demonstrates how powerfully our work systems tend to pull managers away from the shop floor and into their offices where they are isolated from the "gemba".

By formally scheduling a regular time for the manager to be out on the floor (entered as a high priority item on his Outlook calendar) he will have a much better chance of actually getting away from his office. (Some companies designate Gemba Walk time as "sacred time". If this is scheduled throughout the organization at a specific designated time, then even the CEO will learn not to schedule meetings during this sacred time.

Benefit: Bring Together Critical Players to Quickly Solve Problems

It's always hard to get all the critical players together at the same time to review and discuss a problem. We try to do this with regular Production or Staff meetings, but this has a few drawbacks. For one thing, the meetings happen when the information needed is not readily available (as it is on the Visual Metric Board).

During a Gemba walk, all the people are together, they all hear about the problem at the same time, and see the same data. They are therefore all in a position to quickly decide on a course of action, and to initiate that action.

This doesn't work for complex problems, but it does work very well for the most common, nagging problems that are easily solved with a little ingenuity and some good follow-through.

Benefit: Ensure the Metrics Are Valid

By having everyone look at the same metrics, we ensure that those are the metrics we need to be measuring in order to achieve the organization's overall objectives.

For example, if the organization has established a goal to lower scrap costs, but the Visual Metric Board is devoted solely to Productivity and Schedule Attainment, this should be very readily apparent. The manager, who just got beaten up by the VP because scrap costs were 0.1% over budget, will naturally want to know the scrap percentage in each department. If that data is not on the Visual metric board, the manager will then get it added to the board pretty quickly.

Overcoming Pushback

In my experience, Plant Managers who have not already bought into the Gemba Walk process will strongly resist being forced to do them. (I think this is mostly a "control" issue. That's why the Gemba Walk process works best when strongly supported by senior management.) Their objections usually consist of one of the following:

"But I'm already out of the floor all the time anyway"

If so, then a formalized Gemba Walk shouldn't cause them any difficulty. Let's simply formalize what they do now. Pick a single time of day, block out that time on their calendar, invite the supervisors and engineers to this brief period, and they are home free!

Managers love to force hourly associates to do their jobs in a "standard" way. Why not apply the same standard work discipline to the management staff?

"We already have a daily production meeting. This will mean we will talk about the same issues all over again."

A Gemba Walk does have the potential to duplicate a production meeting. The solution is to shorten the existing meeting to focus solely on things that are not applicable to quick discussion on the shop floor. There may be a small amount of overlap, but a well-disciplined production meeting will not duplicate the Gemba Walk very much.

Maybe the daily production meeting can be reduced from 5 days per week to only 2.

"I'm very busy. I don't have time to do a Gemba Walk every day."

Hmmmm. Then how do you know what the heck is going on in your factory? Also, since you are out on the floor all the time, how come you have time for that but not this?

Low level Gemba Walks should happen daily. Higher level walks, by VPs, may happen less often.

"It's too loud on the shop floor to hear anything. We need to meet where we can hear each other."

This can be a real problem. I've solved it in very loud environments by purchasing a hand-held PA system. They are battery powered, fairly lightweight, and usually cost less than £100. That's a pretty small investment considering the benefits you get.

"My people already know what they have to do. They see the Visual Metric Board every day. They don't need me to look at it. Besides, I get the same data emailed to me every day."

You obviously don't buy into the psychological impact of the Lean style of leadership. Managers demonstrate what is important by how they spend their time. If you don't believe this, then nothing I say will change your mind. Good luck!

"I already have a fantastic communication system of voicemails, which I listen to while driving in to work. The communication presented in the Gemba Walk is all a duplicate of what I already know."

This is the strongest of all the pushback arguments I've heard. We don't want to destroy what is already working, but perhaps we can make it better.

Three problems with voicemails are:

1. None of the hourly associates get the voicemails, so they don't know what's going on or what issues are being discussed.
2. Nobody is around to discuss the problem or offer solutions. Everybody hears the message when they are alone, and nobody has the ability to communicate with other team members until after the voicemail is completed. Then they have to remember all the details and contact each team member individually.
3. Nobody sees the manager when he gets the report. They don't pick up on his distress at bad news, or his joy at good news. We lose the entire psychological impact of everyone publicly getting the information at one time.

In this case, I've advised that we pare back the voicemails to bare essentials, such as really good or bad news. This reduces the load on the alternate communication stream and reduces duplicate effort, but still gets us the full benefit of the Gemba Walk process.

How Gemba Walks Fail

Like all Lean procedures, Gemba walks can fail miserably. When they do fail, they make the entire environment worse than it was previously. In my humble opinion, the worst mistake a management team can make is to institute a procedure, and then allow it to slowly fade away. We've all seen this happen, and probably have allowed this to happen many more times than we care to remember.

Lean organizations do "standard work" in almost everything they do. Unfortunately, the natural inclination of people and organizations is to slowly stop adhering to the standards (the 2nd law of thermodynamics works with a vengeance in industrial settings). It takes a tremendous amount of personal energy and discipline to overcome this natural tendency to decay into chaos.

How does the Gemba Walk fail? Here are the usual ways:

Sacred Time isn't so Sacred

The time scheduled for Gemba Walks should be sacred, with everybody who is supposed to be there participating, unless they are either recuperating in the hospital or on vacation.

In my experience, the worst offenders against "sacred time" are senior managers, who will just as quickly chastise you for missing their meeting as demand to know why you are not always doing your Gemba Walks.

Those Smart phones!

We all do it. We can't keep our hands off the smart phones. We check our email every ten seconds, and take every call that comes, no matter what we are doing.

What kind of message does the manager send to the rest of the team when he buries his head in the smart phone while the hourly associate is trying to explain what went wrong the day before? How can he understand what is going on, and give advice and direction if he's replying to an email?

The solution is to turn your smart phone off while on the walk. Better yet, leave it on your desk. You may not realize it, but most smart phones can automatically take a message.

You'll get back to the boss within the hour. I think he can wait.

The Slow Fade-Out

People who are scheduled to be present on the Gemba Walks have other pressing business which keeps them away occasionally. Nobody says anything about their absence, so these conflicts occur more and more often. Eventually, the person comes so rarely that nobody on the Gemba walk even remembers if they ever participated.

To overcome this, the local Lean Champion has to constantly contact the missing people and gently remind them about how critical they are to fixing the problems.

If you find that your presence on the Gemba Walk is not adding value, then say so. Have yourself removed from the schedule. But don't simply stop going.

Chapter 30: Conclusion

Political campaigns are difficult because the candidate must become the person that provides a vision for a wide range of issues to a broad base of constituents. When candidates get into the details, people get lost, bored or they begin hearing things they don't like.

As a result, successful campaigns limit themselves to one message that is used over and over again. "Hope and Change".

If I were to shrink Lean's message into a few words today, I think most would agree it is:

Eliminate Waste

It has all the trappings of success. It is short. It is easy to act on. Everyone wants to remove waste from their process. Unfortunately for Lean, removing waste from a process doesn't necessarily add up to business success.

Lean has a classic campaign problem. Lean has a broad range of concepts, tools and metrics required to be successful. But it only has a short window to communicate to a wide variety of people and an even shorter amount of time to demonstrate success.

So what sound-bite is most frequently absorbed from an introduction to Lean? "Eliminate waste." In fact, to make sure they don't forget this goal, management will post the Seven Wastes of Lean on the wall. Kaizens are held and 5S efforts are not far behind.

175

No surprise at the outcome of this effort. Waste is identified and removed.

"Let the sales team know! We can produce more with no additional labour, equipment or overhead required. Costs are dropping. Finally, we can price aggressively and still make a profit. We'll finally wipe out those pesky low-cost competitors."

All is good

Good, that is, until the competition reacts. They drop their prices to meet yours. At that point, volume begins dropping. With all this extra capacity, idle people and machines stick out like sore thumbs. I don't have to tell you what happens next.

Is it any wonder many people consider Lean a failed methodology? It results in lay-offs and shrinks the revenue opportunity. It is now harder to survive than before Lean was introduced.

While reducing waste is a great objective and simple message, there is a fundamental problem with it. It doesn't tell people what to do with that extra capacity. As a result, some companies will inadvertently have it work against them. If I were Lean's campaign advisor, this would be the new campaign message:

Reduce Lead Time

I can still use the basic tools such as kaizen, 5S and even hang a poster. The difference is I am only going to focus on those things that will reduce lead time.

More importantly, I know what to do with any gains that I earn: Reduce lead time.

This is important for three reasons: It works with existing metrics, shorter lead times are a sustainable competitive advantage. Finally, companies can cash that buffer, time, in for a wide variety of benefits. Let's look at this in more detail.

First, reducing lead times will work with the current metrics in place at any company. Have a Lean related success? Change the lead time on the master data screen in your ERP system. Every other metric will continue to work. If you are not willing to change the lead time then it doesn't count as a success.

Second, Start quoting shorter lead times rather than reducing prices. Give your customer that time as an additional value. They will hungrily chew it up with their own inefficiency or use it to make themselves more competitive. And you will still get the satisfaction of nailing the competition. When they have to meet your lead time or lose an order, the competition will use overtime and premium freight to overcome their inefficiencies. Fists will start thumping on tables because both are immediate red flags. Management knows profits or volume will soon fall but no answer is in sight.

Third, a shorter lead time gives you more options to manage your business. Removing waste scatters benefits throughout the plant making it difficult to cash in. A shorter lead time puts all the efficiencies in one place; time at the tail end of the process.

If increased volume isn't your goal, you can cash that time in for a wide variety of benefits. For example, move overseas operations closer to your customers. This will allow you create jobs at higher wages because you can eliminate logistics costs.

Enter new markets with no capital investment. Get rid of that last bit of Overtime and Premium freight. Or invest the time back into more improvements.

Lean manufacturing has become one of the most widely used and popular manufacturing methods. More and more manufacturing businesses are using lean manufacturing to cut costs and improve the efficiency of their production process.

There are many different benefits to using lean manufacturing which has led many businesses to see that using lean manufacturing will help them to stay competitive in an ever growing competitive market. Savvy manufacturing business owners are learning all they can about this highly beneficial process that allows them to run their manufacturing business with the highest degree of efficiency and lowest cost possible.

Best of all the use of lean manufacturing has been shown to provide the means for producing a product that is higher in quality while remaining lower in cost.

Good luck!

Resource and References

Shigeo Shingo, Norman Bodek, Collin McLoughlin: Kaizen and the Art of Creative Thinking - The Scientific Thinking Mechanism

Shigeo Shingo; Fundamental Principles of Lean Manufacturing

Shigeo Shingo, Andrew P. Dillon (Translator); Zero Quality Control: Source Inspection and the Poka-yoke System

Shigeo Shingo; Non-Stock Production: The Shingo System of Continuous Improvement

Shigeo Shingo; A Study of the Toyota Production System from an Industrial Engineering Viewpoint

Shigeo Shingo; A Study of the Toyota Production System from an Industrial Engineering Viewpoint

Drucker, P. (1993) Post-Capitalist Society

Drucker, P., "What Makes an Effective Executive", Harvard Business review, June 2004

Lessons from Toyota's long drive, an interview with Katsuaki Watanabe, HBR, July 2007

Liker, J. & D. Meier, Toyota Talent, McGraw Hill, 2007

Shook, J. , Managing To Learn, Lean Enterprise Institute 2008

Fishman, C., "No Satisfaction", Fast Company, Dec 2006/Jan 2007

Womack, J. & J. Shook, Lean Management and The Role of Lean Leadership, Lean Enterprise Institute presentation, Oct. 2006